Hyper Effigy
Brian Getnick

General Projects
April 3 - May 30, 2021

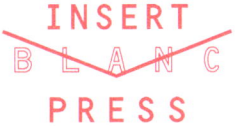

Los Angeles

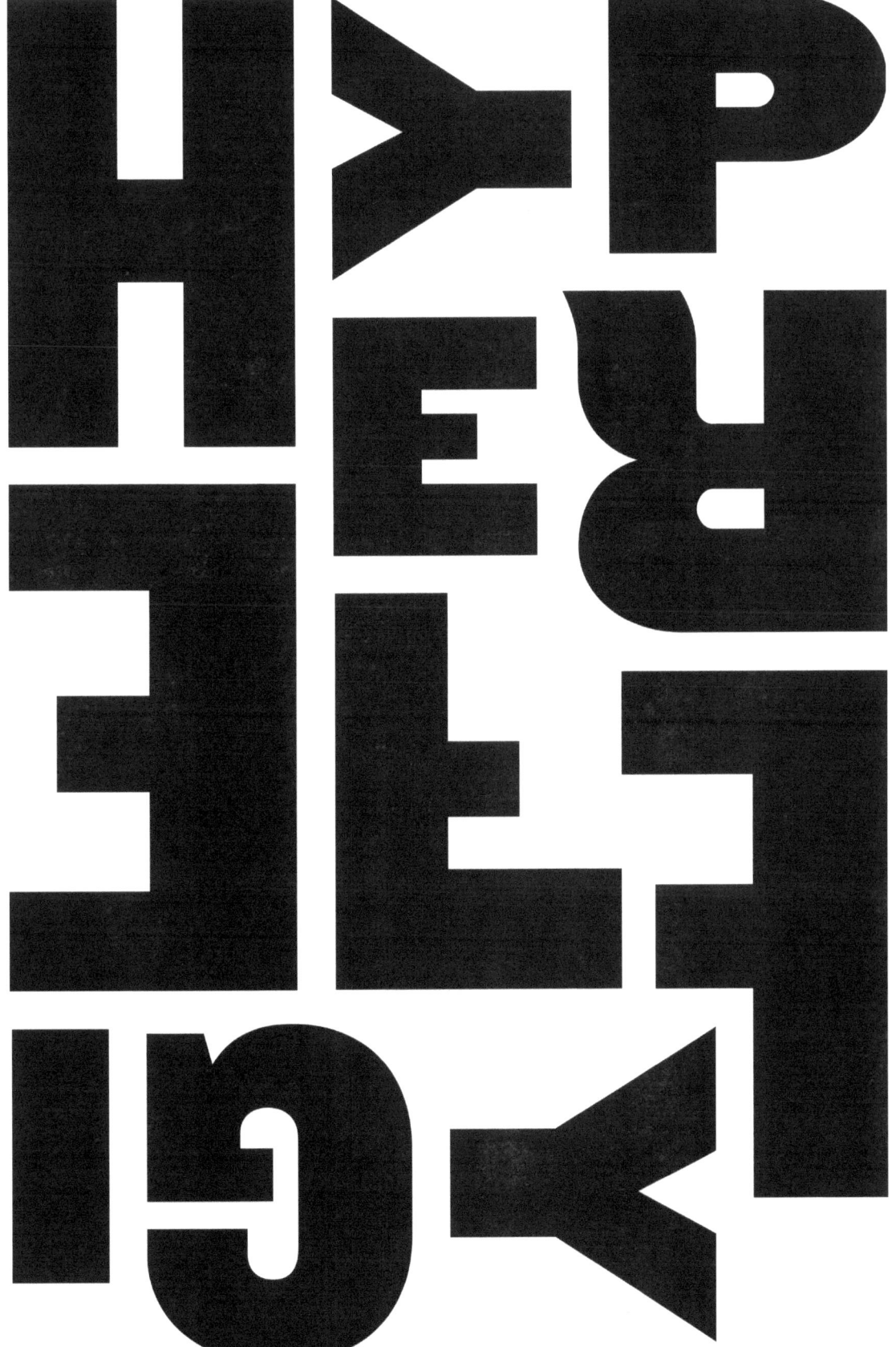

Hyper Effigy

© 2021 Brian Getnick

Insert Blanc Press

ISBN : 978-1-947322-07-3

Cover design Dameon Waggoner

Photographic Documentation David Weldzius

Stills from the performance of *Secret Joy*
at Human Resources Los Angeles 2019
Julie Weitz and Ian Byers Gamber

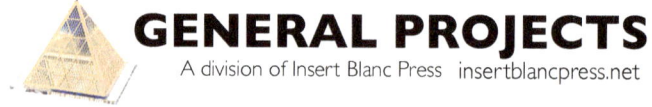

"These characters, I say, present themselves. They have not been whipped into place. As though it were the most natural thing in the world, they denounce themselves..."

-Elias Canetti

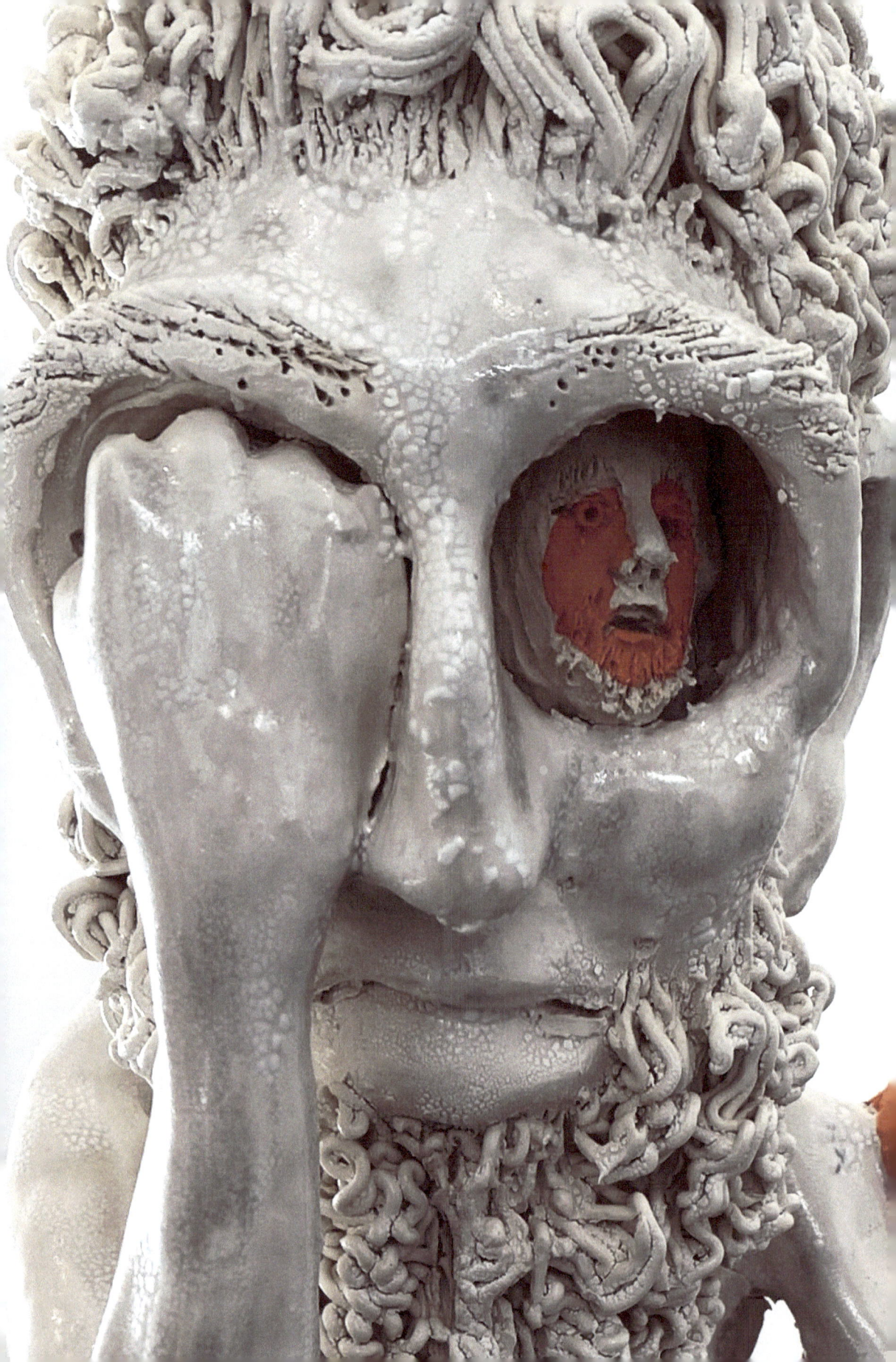

Introduction Mathew Timmons	9
Hyper Effigy Grace Hadland	13
Hyper Effigy Brian Getnick General Projects	19
Abyss Standard	31
Works on Paper	51
Ersatz Fighting Unit	61
Sculptural Props from *Secret Joy* Outside Gallery	73
Secret Joy performance script	83
Press Release and Index of Works	97

Introduction
Mathew Timmons

Towards the end of 2020 I found myself thinking over the work I had seen over the past few years that really stuck with me. The one name that kept coming to the top of my mind was Brian Getnick.

I run **Insert Blanc Press**, which supports work that reaches across mediums and disciplines and, among other things, produces catalogs documenting shows at **General Projects** and **Outside Gallery**, the gallery and exhibition space I built in a former garage next to my home in Lincoln Heights, and I also co-host an arts and literary podcast, **The People**, while maintaining my own writing practice and getting up to various other things in the meantime. If all these projects sound like the burden of a pathological multitasker, you probably don't live in Los Angeles where this type of work within and for the arts community is a long tradition, one that Getnick and I both come from.

While working on this show I reacquainted myself with all the reasons Brian's name kept coming to mind. I picked up the first issue of the performance art journal **NS** (**Native Strategies**) he did in collaboration with Tanya Rubbak, and read this gem:

> I thought of it as a catalog of sorts but what it ended up being is still the format that we work with, which is a tool for hunting the core critical perspectives within artists' practices. I guess that's one of the most important things about Native Strategies—that it's asserting that artists already have richly researched critical frameworks, and if we're going to look at the full spectrum of what performance art is in Los Angeles, it's best to start by talking to the artists themselves.
> —Brian Getnick, **NS #1 So Funny It Hurts**

At some point we decided Getnick's show **Hyper Effigy** would open at **General Projects** over Easter weekend and as time passed the world slowly opened up, more people got vaccinated and we all experienced a collective revival of some kind. Calendrical happenstance made Getnick's show into a resurrection of everything I wanted to keep from the art world encapsulated by the quote above: artists centering each other.

Let's do one quick rewind to late September 2019. I went with a couple people to see Getnick's production, **Secret Joy**, at **Human Resources** in Chinatown. I had seen Brian relatively recently, even stopped by his studio and began to marvel at everything going on there, but really it had been a while, and so I was completely electrified by what I saw at **Human Resources** that night. I loved the grand-stand bleachers arranged in a semicircle, like we were there to witness a Roman Bloodsport. I loved the monumentality of the vaguely constructivist set pieces and the range the performers conveyed through their sheer physicality and as they exchanged and repeated the broken text which is reprinted towards the back of this book.

In Getnick's exhibition **Hyper Effigy**, sculptural props from that performance are exhibited in **Outside Gallery**. The night of the opening, visitors insisted they take up the red cudgel and take a whack at the big blue head. Getnick didn't stop them, even when cracks were revealed in the

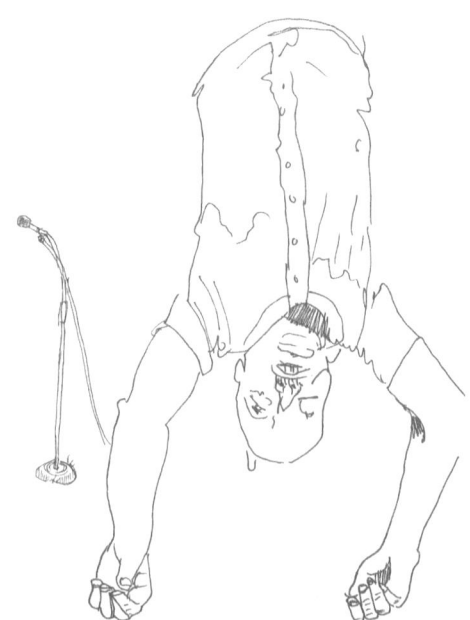

monstrous jaw and cheek, he seemed unphased. Indeed, this type of rough play is fundamental to how he conceives of flipping the reality of props (objects typically prop up a performance) and instead allowing the performance to create the object. His sculptures designed for performance are engineered to allow the narrative and physical flow of a performance to modify the reality of the object. Quite literally, breaking it is part of making it. Between performances he mends the damage and the sculpture transforms. Violence is the subtractive process and the subsequent repair is the additive process. "There is a hardiness that I want out of my work; it's got to withstand somebody like Alice Cvnt working inside of it," he says.[1]

As Brian was working on a follow up performance to **Secret Joy**, covid quarantine life took over, and he, like the rest of us, had to stop and find an outlet for his ideas that didn't involve gathering people. Getnick returned to the ceramics studio of the school where he teaches and shifted his creative energy from performance into the object. During our initial, virtual studio visit I encountered a skeleton with a violinist crouched between its bowed legs, a troll with a small face peering out of an oversized eye socket, and what looked to be a Roman senator's bust astride a reptilian beast. Beyond their fantastical appearance their presence was raw, emotional, and vulnerable.

The figures I first encountered in our studio visit were from Getnick's series **Abyss Standard**, seven ceramic figures, arranged in a circle like sentinels peering out over a chest high wooden disk. Each figure named after a day of the week and morphologically distinct, but unified in their arm's length scale and their color—bubbly white, dry grey and lashed with electric orange. They evoke classical figures, the Roman bust or the Kouros—a stylized youth placed at the head of ancient tombs. Like the Kouros, the characters of the Abyss seem to be markers of our time, small memorials to daily death tolls in the news and in our personal lives.

Abyss Standard evokes ceramics as a system of noticing

---

[1] Alice Cvnt is a performance maker and artist who worked frequently with Getnick in the early aughts.

and marking death and time that develops through traditions in sculpture: the trollish, demonic baroque, the artifact, kitsch. I wouldn't want to degrade these talismans by calling them kitsch and yet kitsch can't be avoided when cherubs, trolls and skeletons are present. It's a term that demarks emotional space the art world tells us to avoid as a matter of good, austere and cynical taste.

Getnick's cosmology is emotional, magical, and avoids the dichotomy of emotion vs. value. **Abyss Standard** greets you as you walk into **General Projects**, a heptagonal marker of time, day by day, a cosmogony or mythological calendar of personal significance.

As Getnick says:

> Without performance I had to ask, who do my objects face? Pandemic time was time freed up from the responsibility of speaking towards an art world audience that had gone dark, gone silent. In that silence I felt guidance from the mere fact that I was still compelled to create these figures, impossible to do in a vacuum, a void that sucks at you, but easy in the void that remains when a pressurized image of the world fabricated by your goals, your opportunities, your ambitions is swept away by a virus.
>
> There were presences, I won't say a "who" or a "what," but a conscious force, not mine, somewhere in that pressure between my fingers and the clay. I realized I could just keep working like this, in the abyss, dredging up a report from that open dark space.
> The **Abyss Standard** is like that: day to day reportage from refreshingly dark interstitial space.

Hyper Effigy
Grace Hadland

A husband living in the postwar suburbs of New England, encounters a woman he recognizes at a dinner party. He struggles to place her. After asking the hostess where she was from, a small village in France, his memory is jogged. She had been the subject of a public shaming spectacle after the war. During the Occupation, she lived with the Nazis. In an act of performative revenge and humiliation for her participation with the Germans, the townspeople shaved her head and stripped her of her clothes then forced her out of the village naked and alone. An audience watched and jeered, the husband among them with his cohort of American soldiers. The scene comes from John Cheever's 1954 story "The Country Husband," capturing the lull and alienation of interwar suburban life. The nature of power is revealed to be perverse and fickle when time acts as a catalyst for its shifting dynamics. The reversal of roles, shifting of power is often disorienting and unsettling.

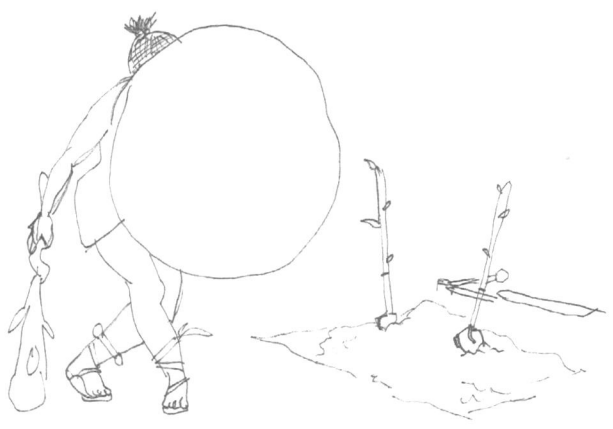

Brian Getnick evokes and mimics the monumentality of public shrines to state power and/or dissenters. The figures assume an ambiguous position between both authority and subject, the distinction between the two is attempted to be explicit but unravels. In this way, his sculptural figures hone in on the choreography of exchanging power, questioning the stability of the categories they establish of victim and perpetrator. In Ersatz Fighting Unit (all works 2020) two figures face each other, Soldier and Counter Soldier, their opposition only disclosed with the addition of "counter" without it they are both just soldiers. One is in red, one in blue, but the blue is deep yet not navy and the red is slightly too purple for public uniforms. The Counter Soldier in red, possibly a revolutionary wears a balaklava adorned with a bauble on top. The knitted texture of the mask is porous and almost revealing. Opposing the masked figure is a blue bust with a helmet adorned with some organic flourish. In the final element of the series of ceramic pieces, the figures become one. Soldier / Counter Soldier merge as if a ceramic portmanteau. The counter soldier's neck becomes the soldier's head, one upside down, one right side up, suggesting a cyclical motion of reversal. The work has the silhouette of an hourglass, as if to be turned once time is up. The effigies Getnick proposes are two faced, two headed like a greek god whose duality is both his divine advantage and curse. Have they merged, or have they always been one?

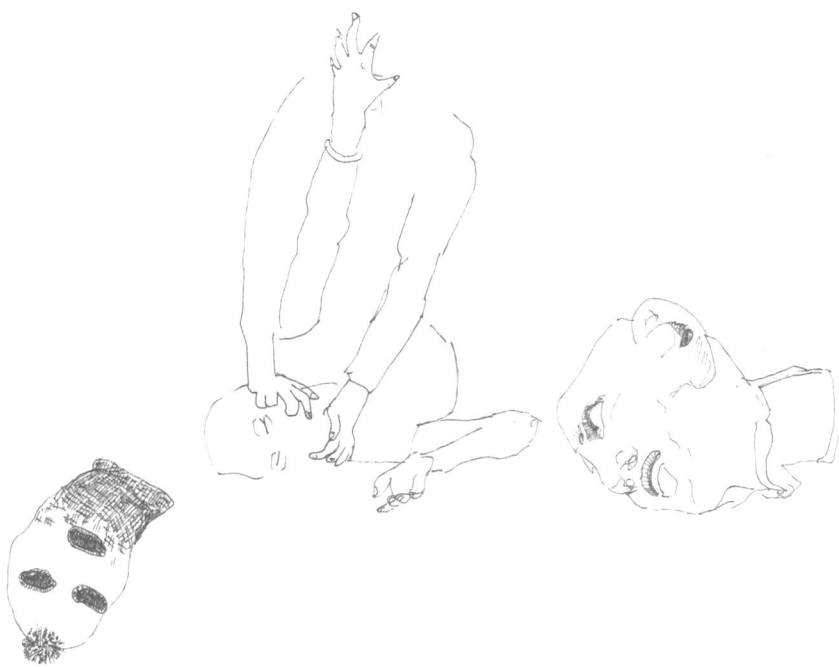

At the dinner party, the woman bends over to refill the husband's cocktail and serve him his dinner. She's the maid employed by the hosts of the dinner party. As time has passed, the relationship has shifted between the husband and the maid; their roles have been reversed and reversed again. In his memory, she is simultaneously victim and perpetrator, punished for a past of violence (is this justice?). The husband then assumes the role of power to her subordinate position, the role of guest to her position as servant. The banality of that moment, of domestic service at a dinner party the husband does not want to be at, is almost irreconcilable with the brutality and violence intertwined with his memory of the woman as a prisoner of war.

Cheever writes, "The people in the Farquarsons living room seemed united in their tacit claim that there had been no past, no war— that there was no danger or trouble in the world." Cheever illustrates a kind of cultural amnesia, a Protestant response to a trauma that is too difficult to reckon with or reflect upon. A similar phenomenon has dominated contemporary political discussions following the 2020 US election. The categories of victim/perpetrator are constantly reinforced in the realm of political spectacle, it has become the primary mode of identification. Coming out of a moment of hysteria, many are united in a desire to forget, to abandon the past and hang their values onto hollow categories of right and wrong.

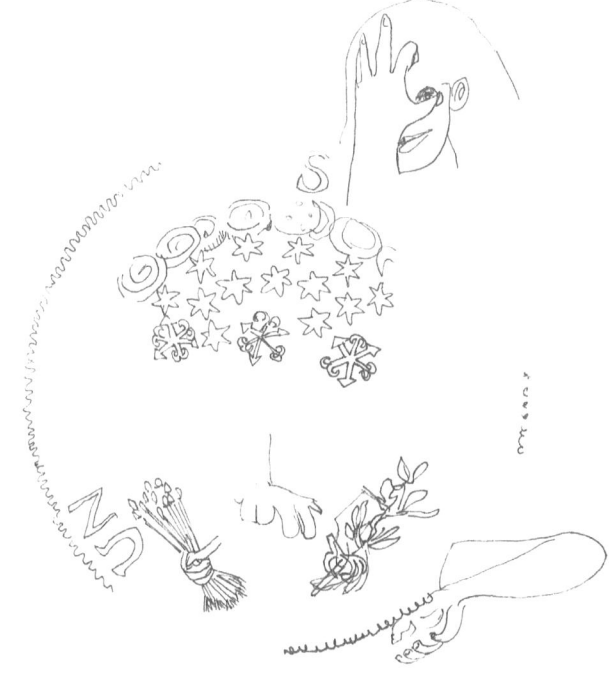

Getnick dwells on the visual representation of these categories, how distinctions are made through sartorial or physical adornments. These categories have been incorporated into every identity; they are tossed back and forth, taken on and off like a coat and hat. In Cheever's story, the retribution for violence is to be stripped and shaved. To be stripped of one's clothes and hair, no longer armored with a costume that affirms one's identity, one's position in society is the ultimate punishment. To be a blank body in public is considered the proper retribution for unbearable atrocities. Without a shield of sartorial identity, the individual is rendered weak. The ceramics' hollowness, the holes and cracks in Getnick's forms remind the viewer of how flimsy and sheer the exterior really is.

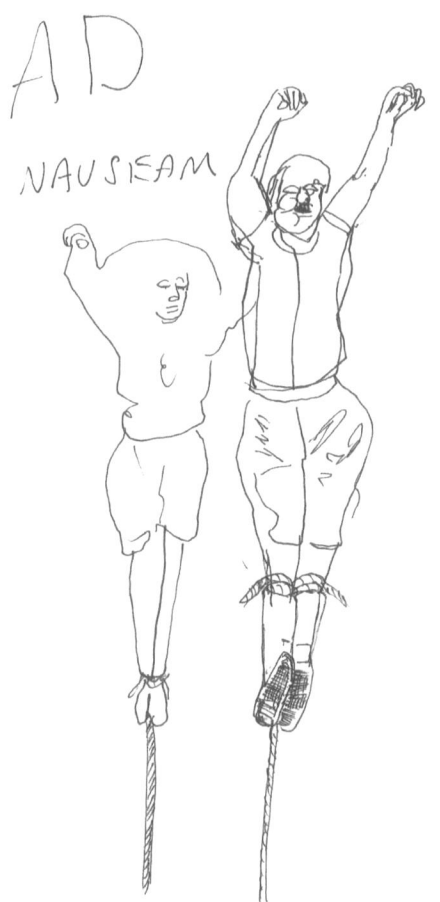

The husband in Cheever's story remembers the scene of public chastisement and that at one point the cheering subsided: "The jeering ended gradually put down by the recognition of a common humanity." This commonality, the shared experience of being human and the recognition of it is what seems constant in the vague liberal, centrist affirmations of 'world peace' or 'unity.' For Getnick and Cheever, however, this common humanity is more insidious, less likely to offer a positive point of unity than to carry the lurking threat of a cudgel.

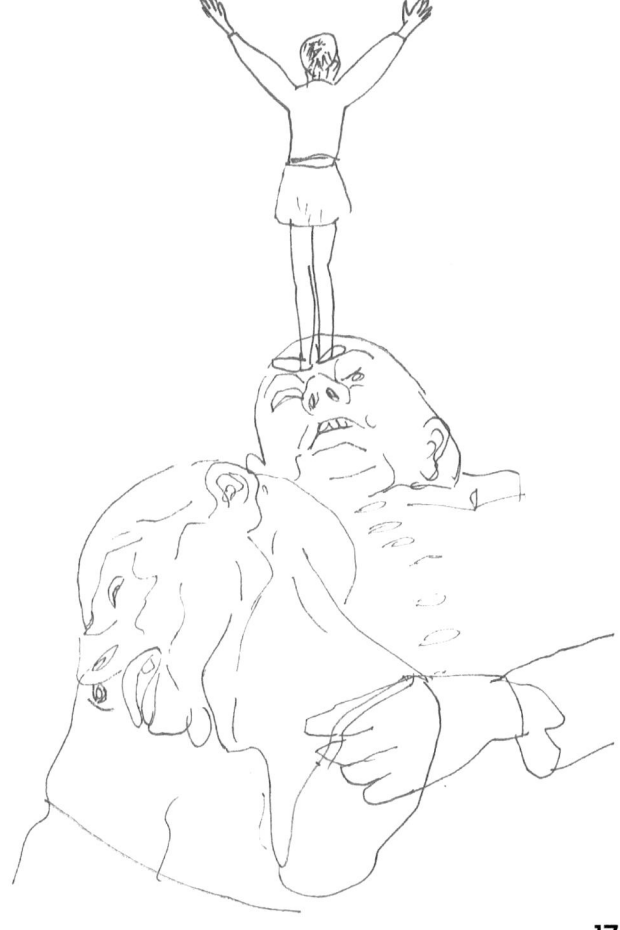

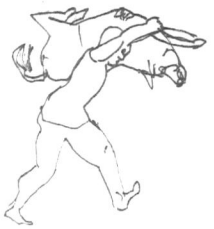

Hyper Effigy
Brian Getnick

General Projects
April 3 - May 30, 2021

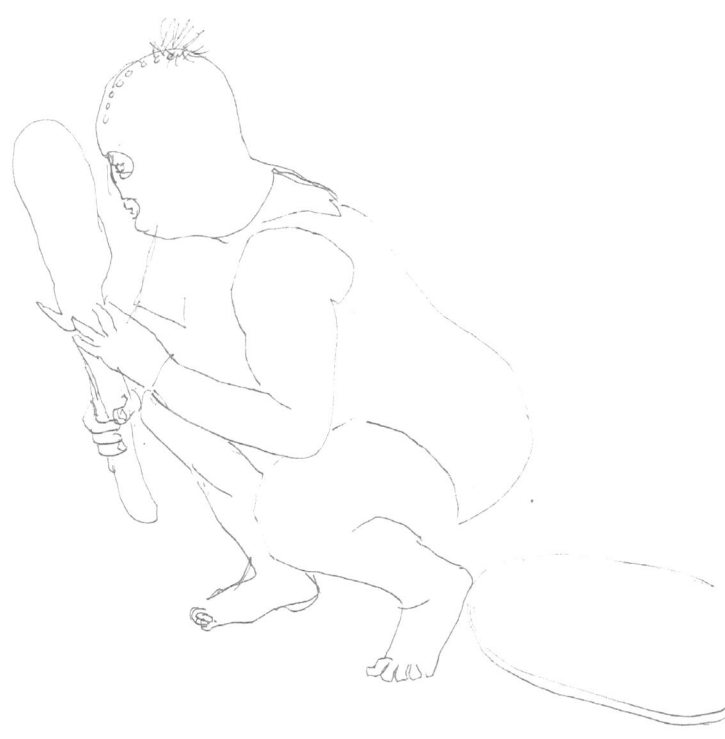

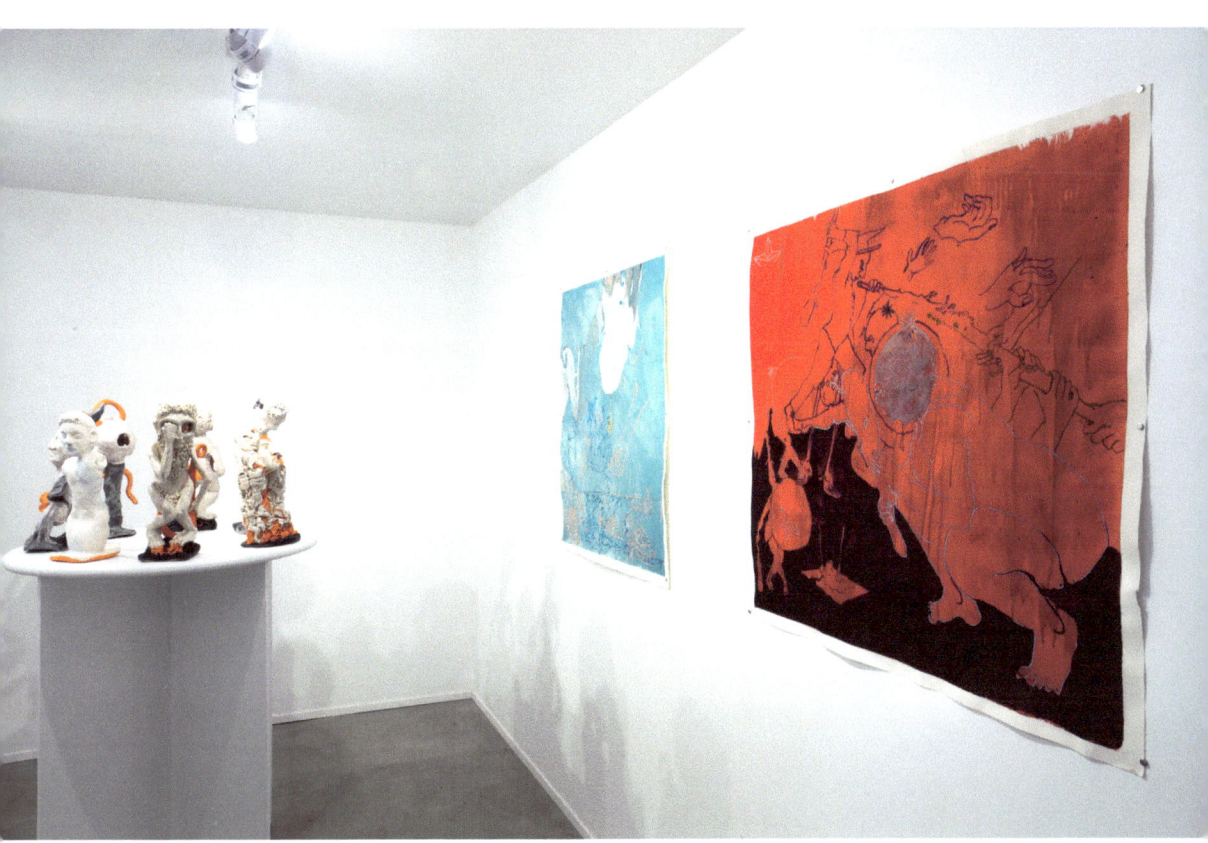

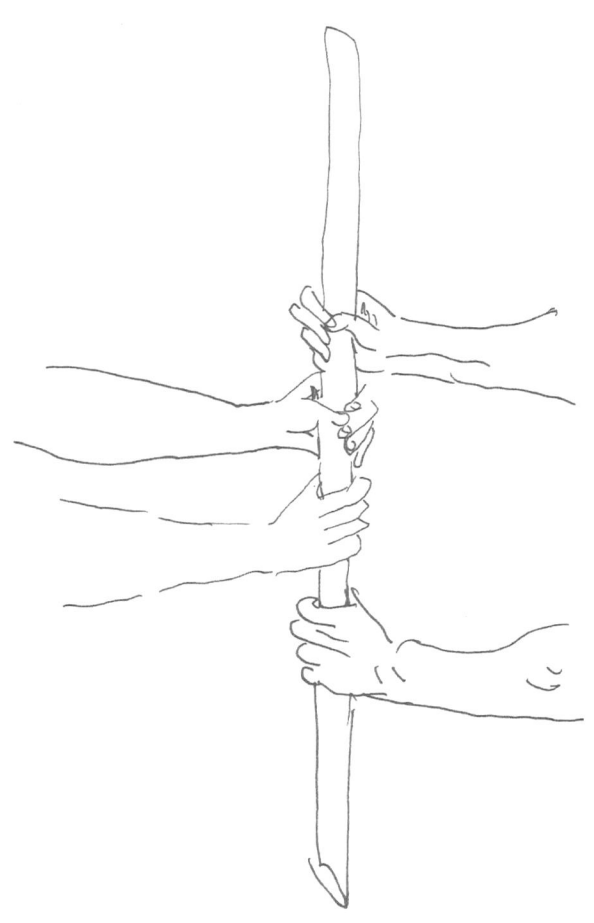

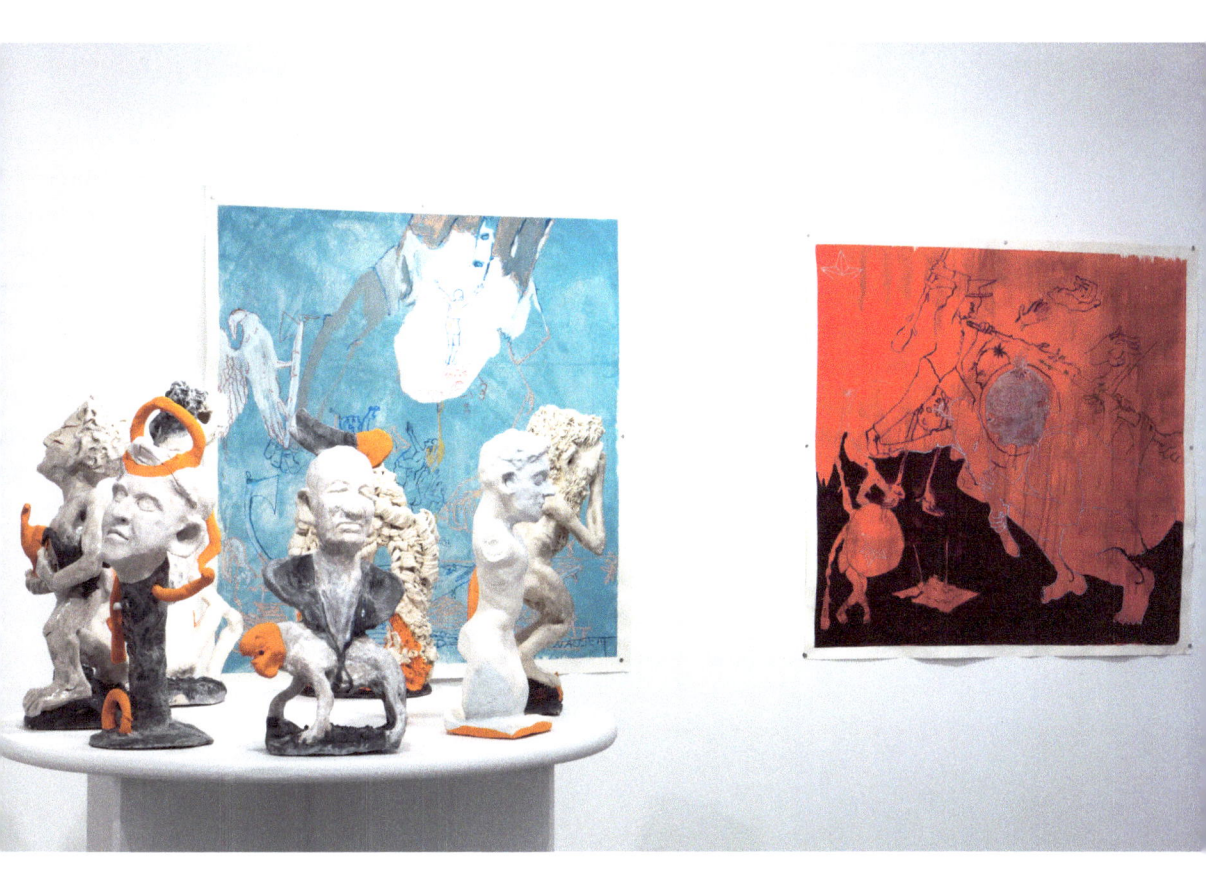

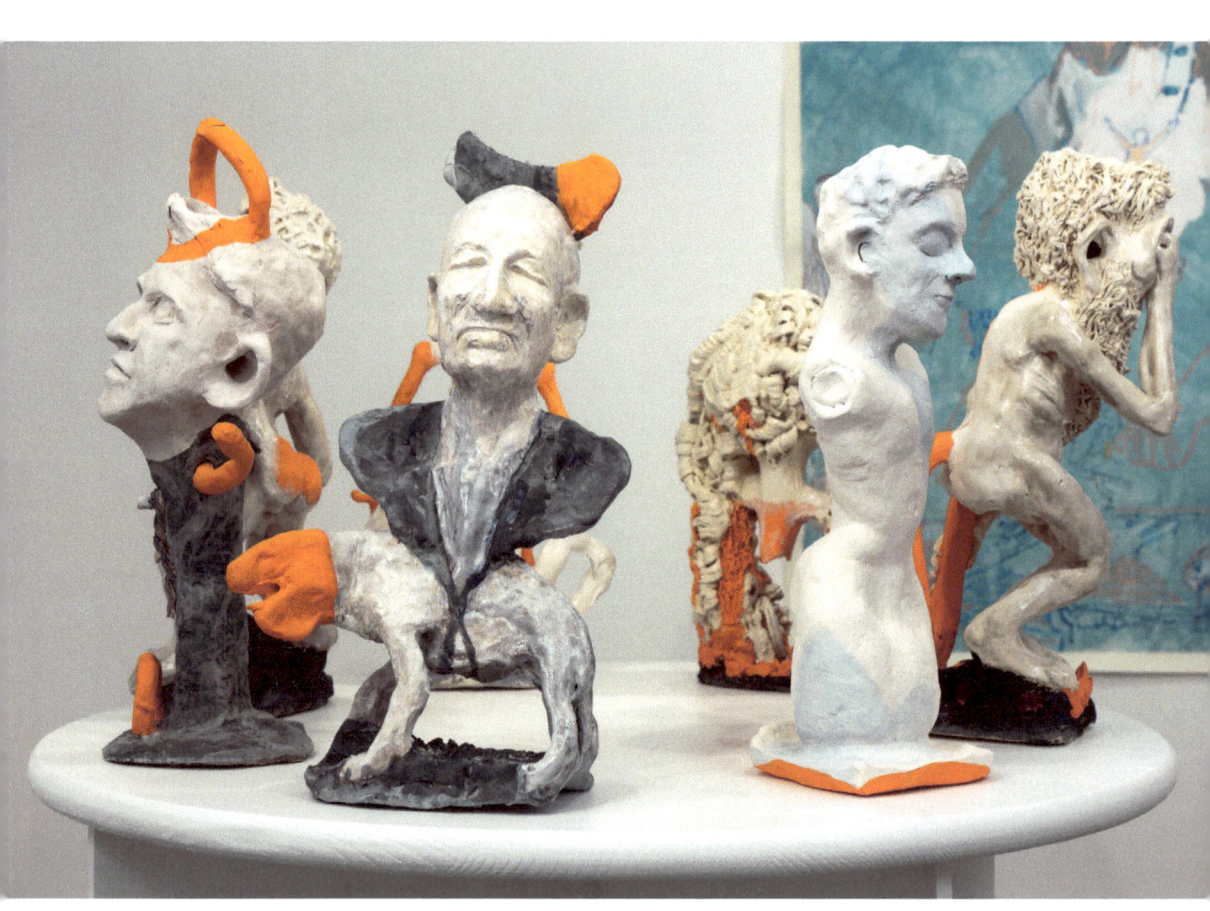

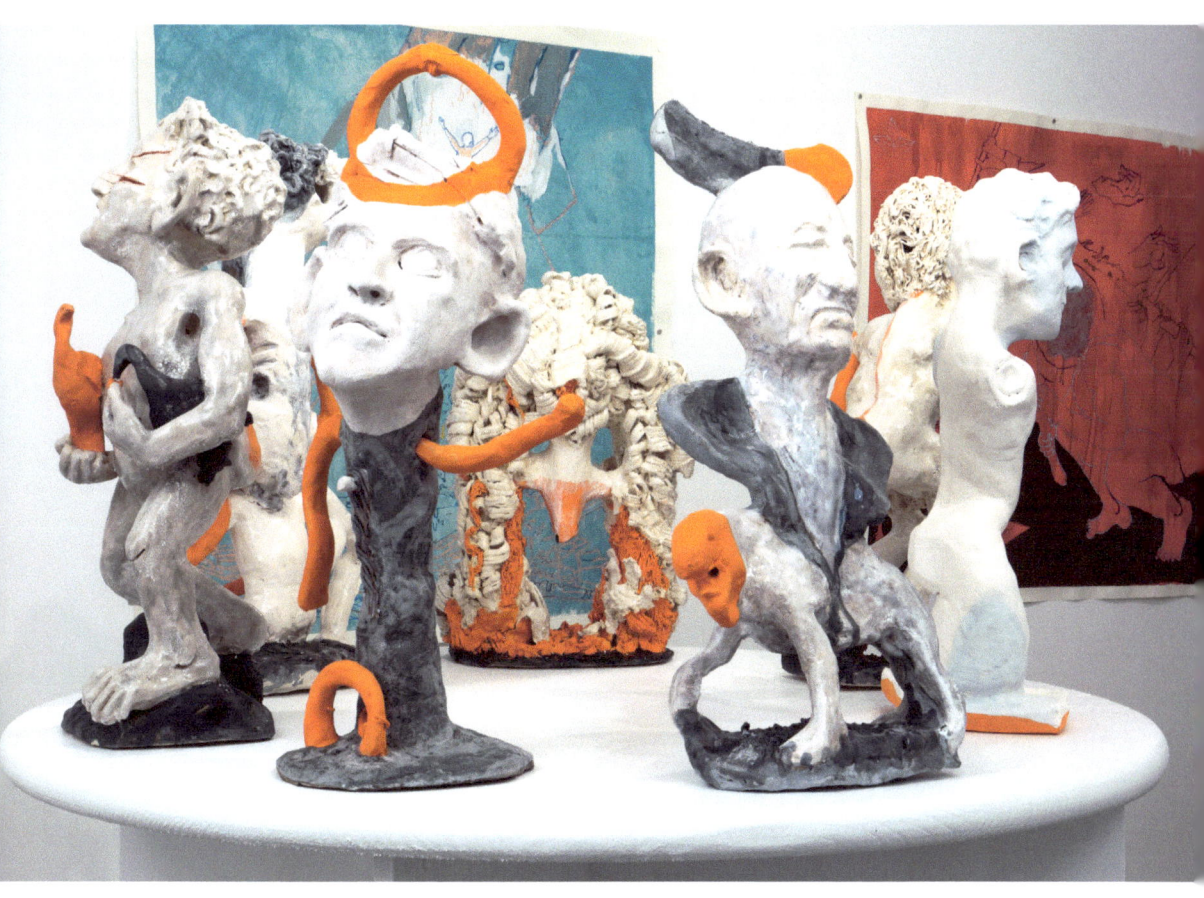

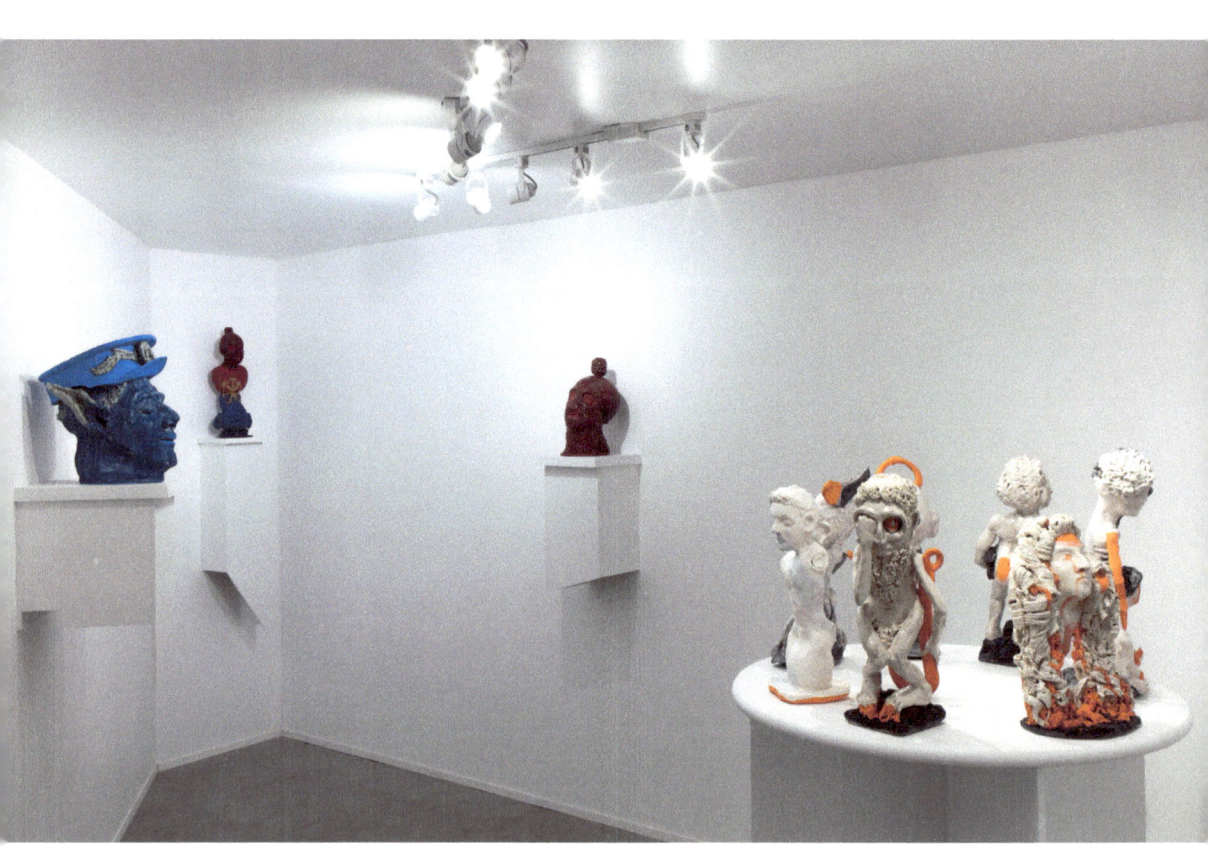

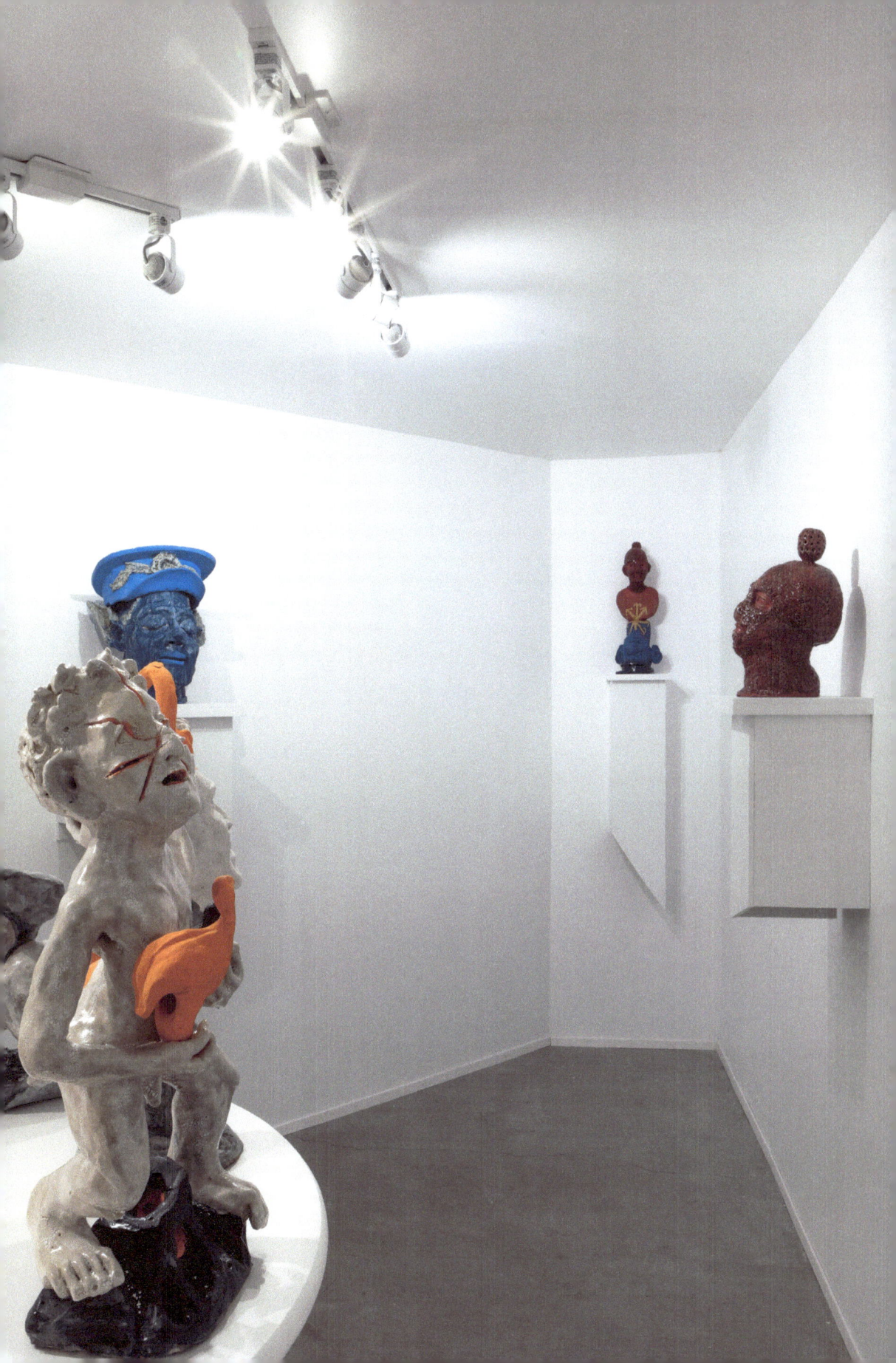

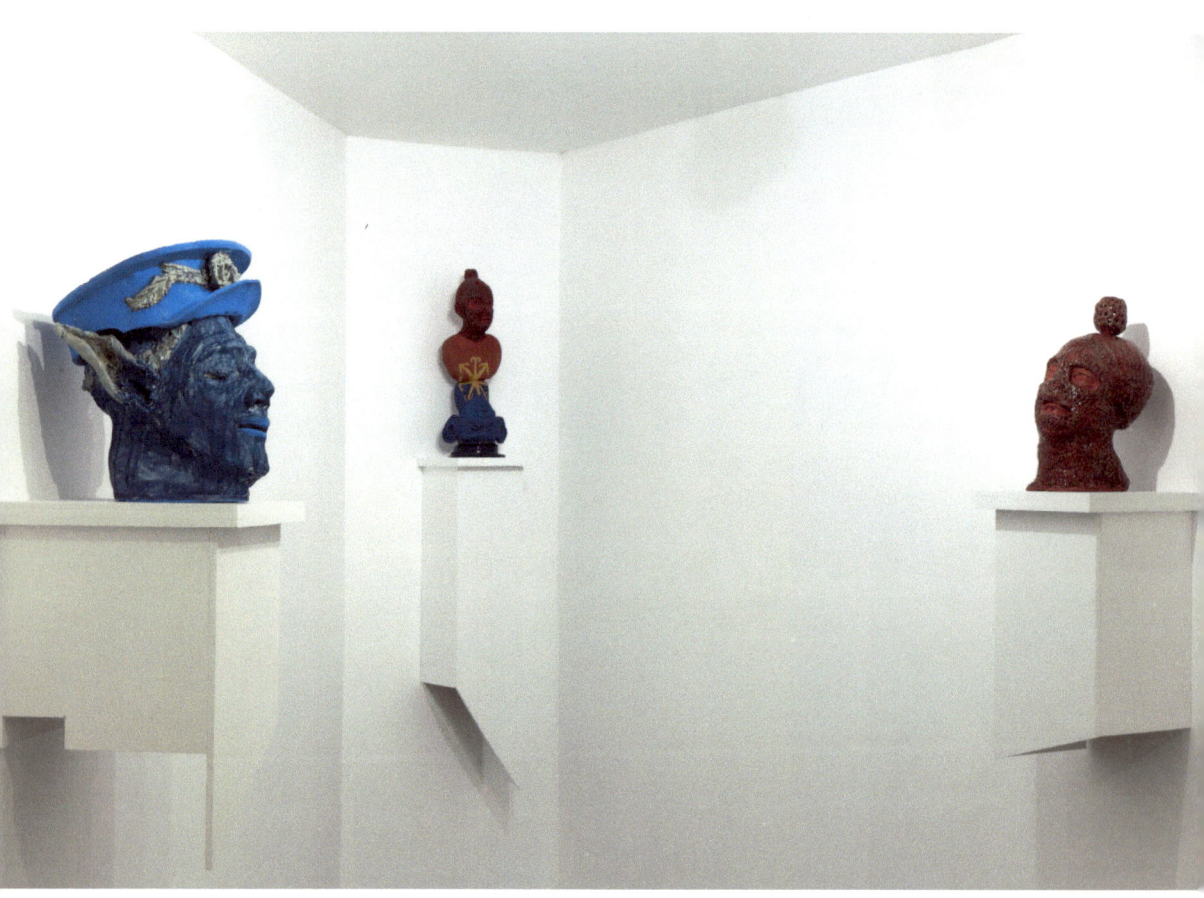

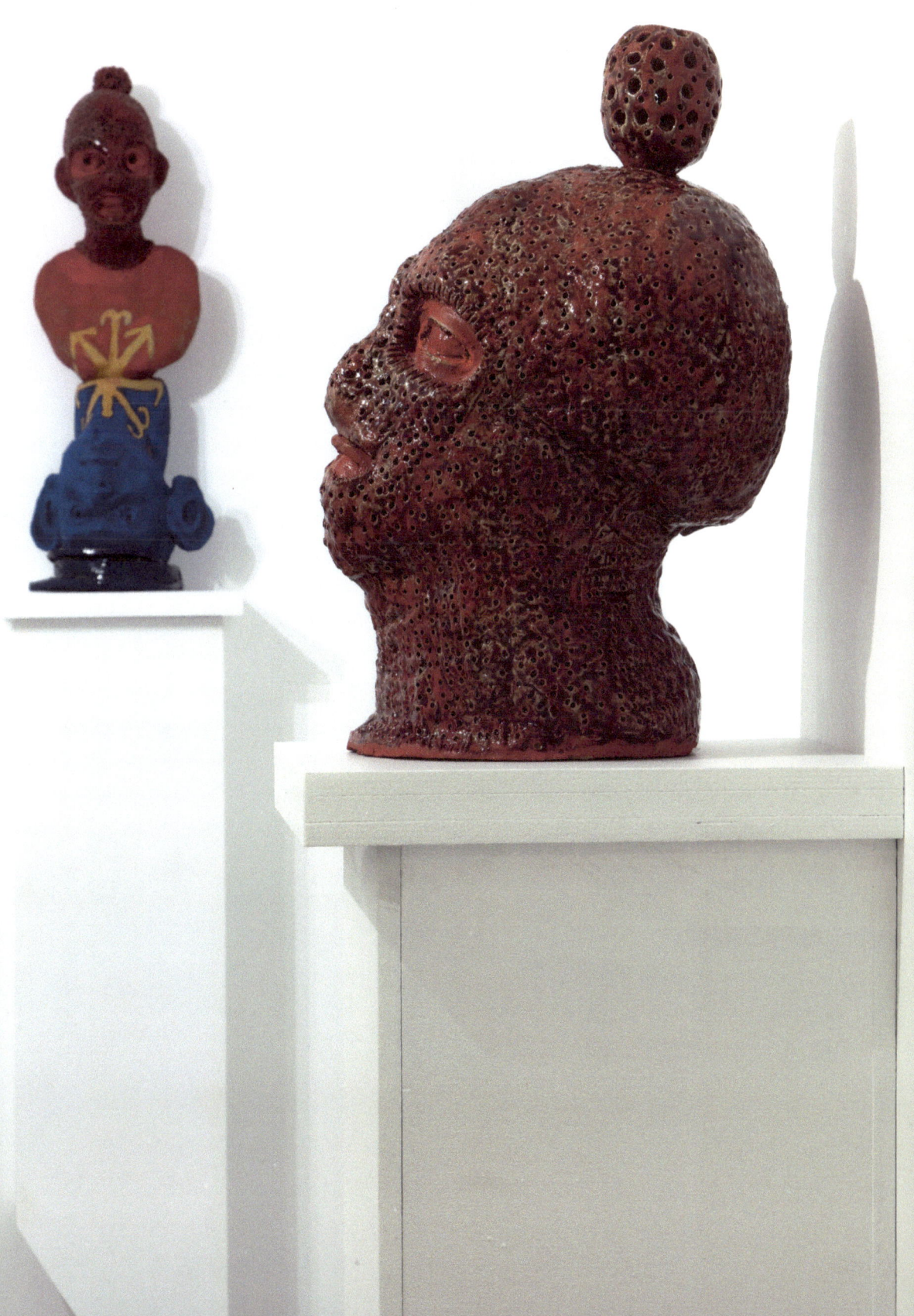

Abyss Standard Hyper Effigy

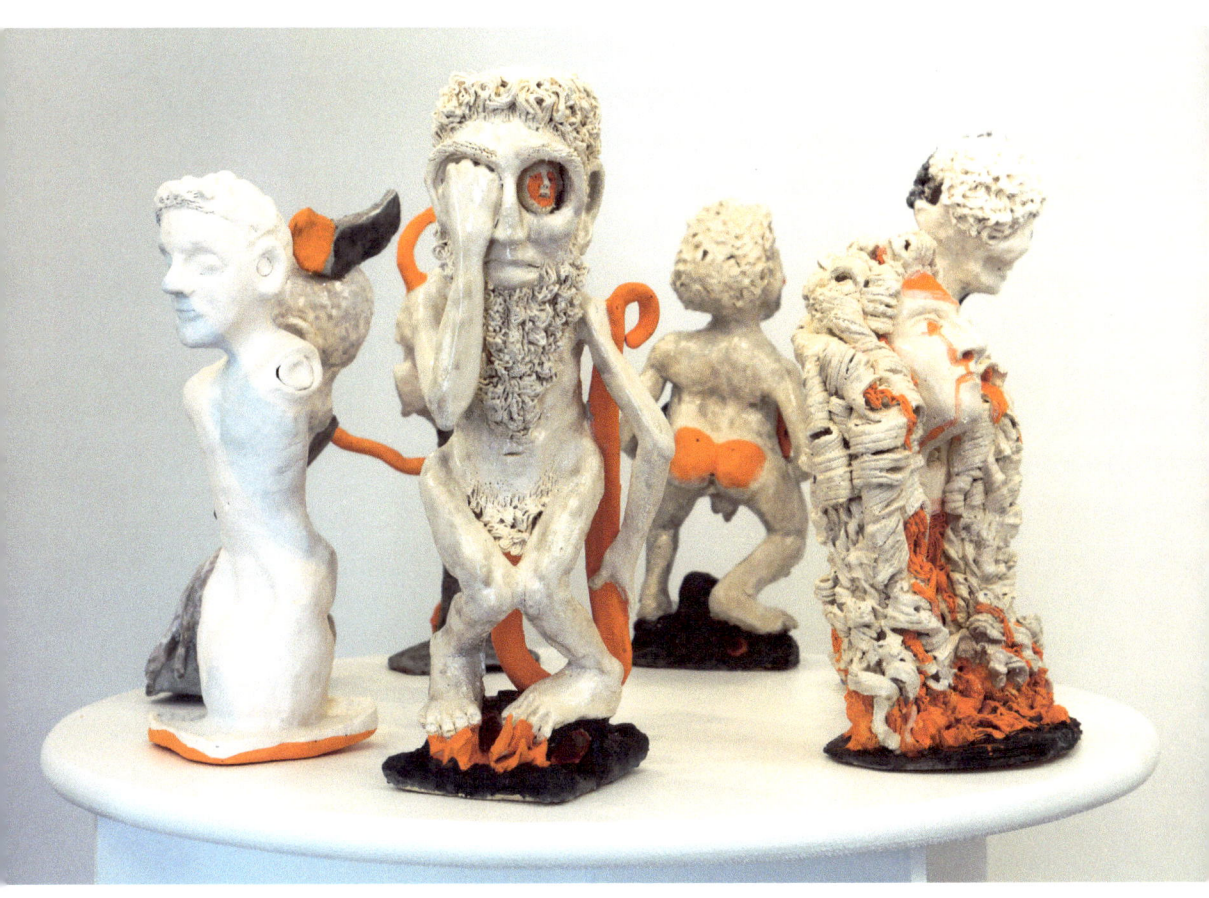

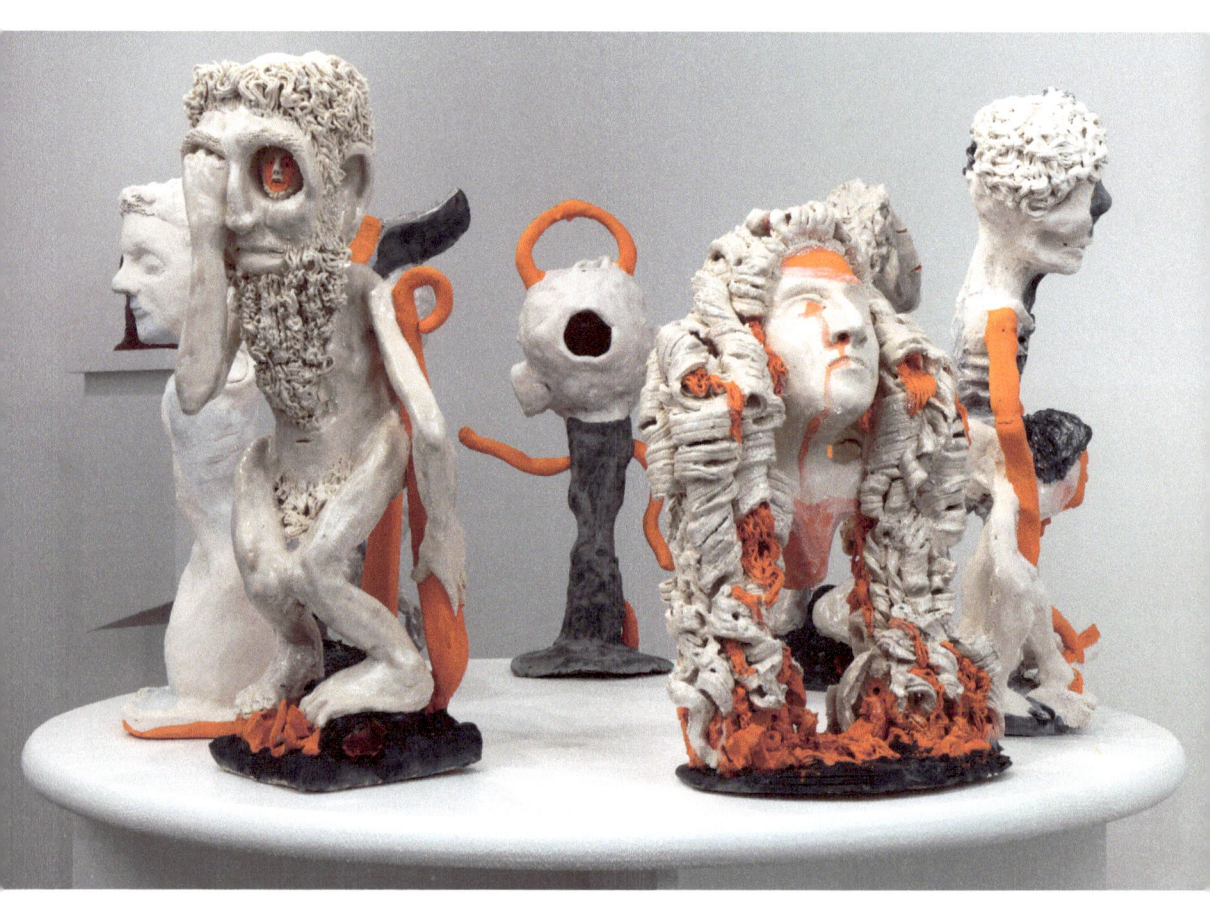

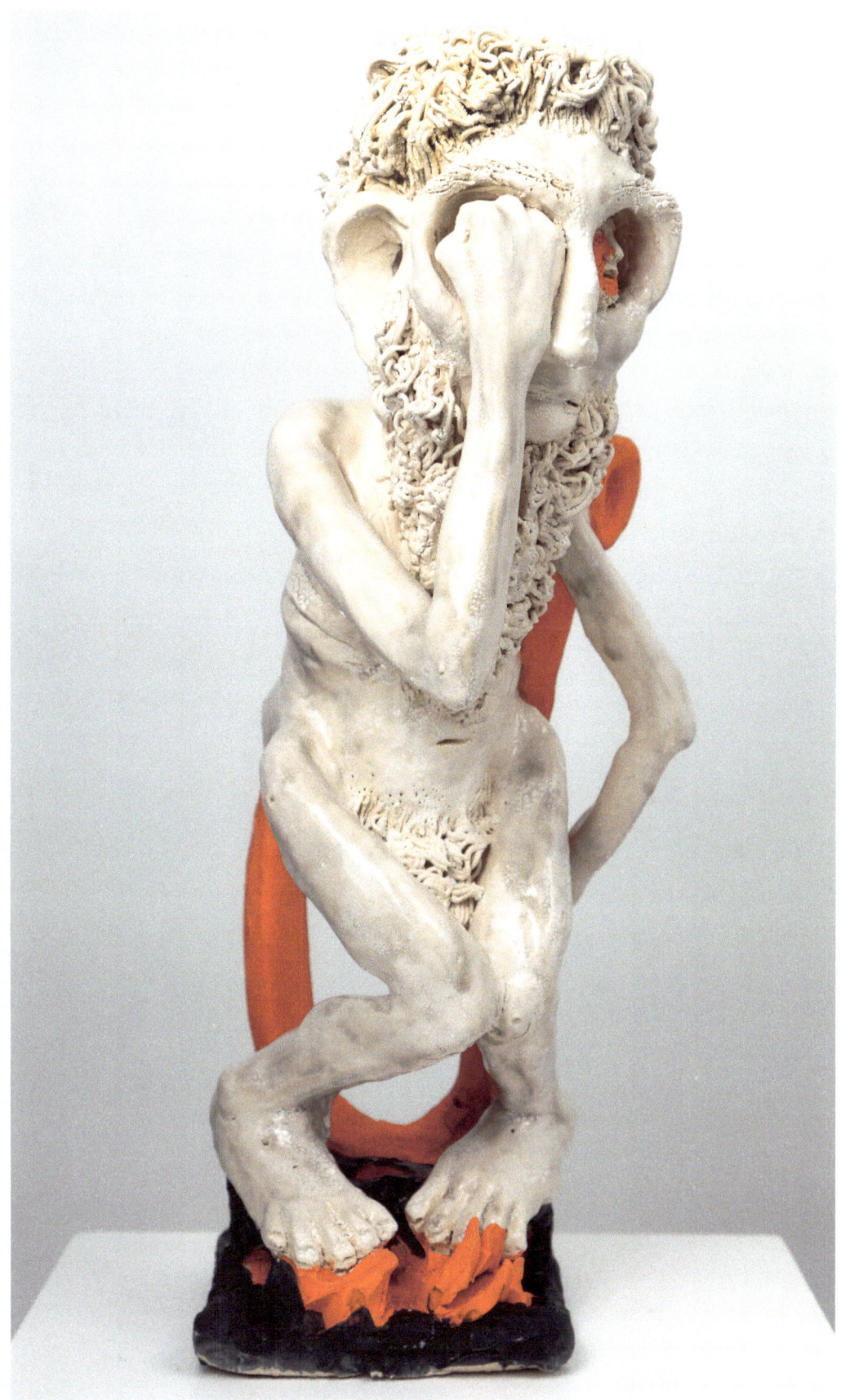

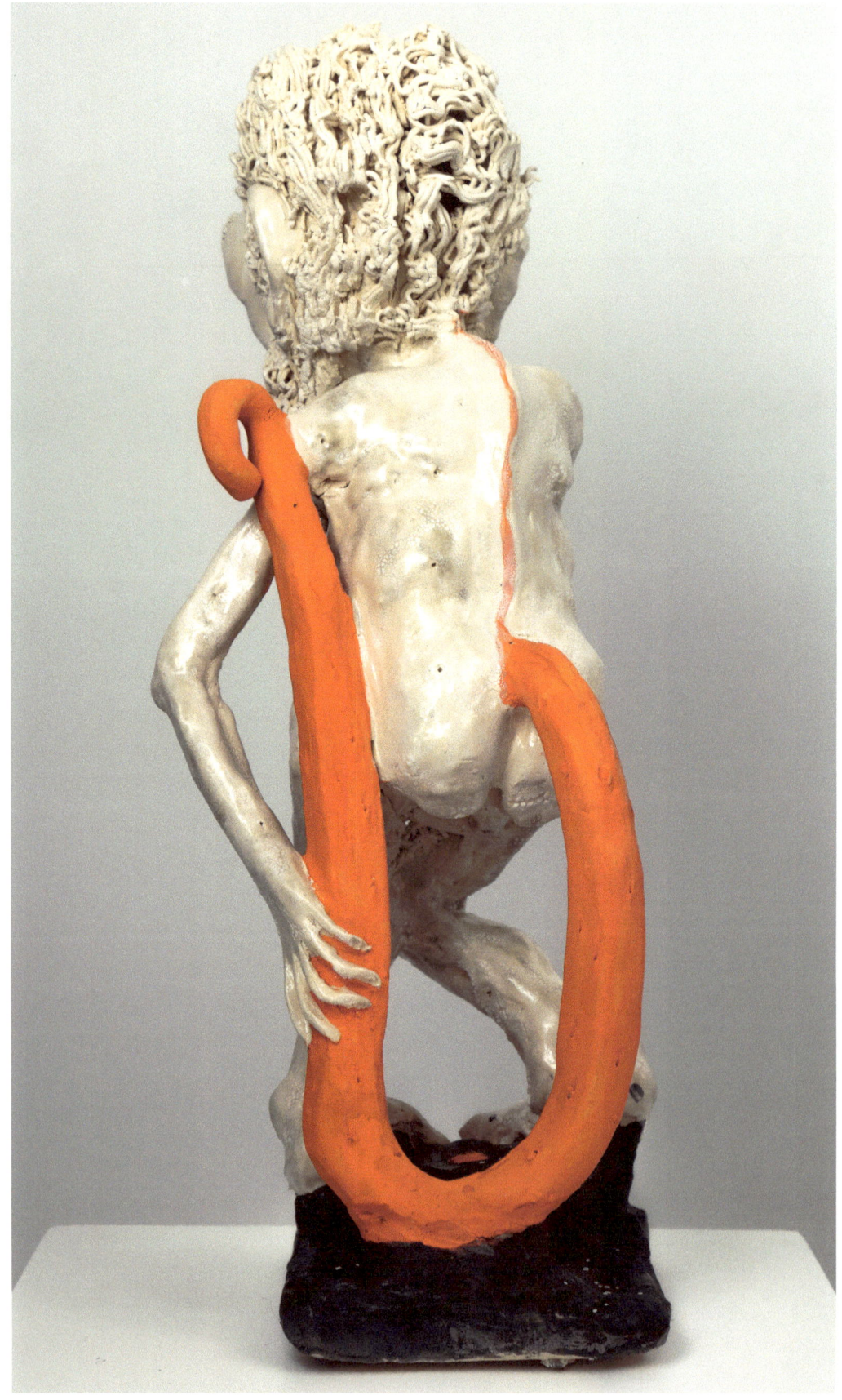

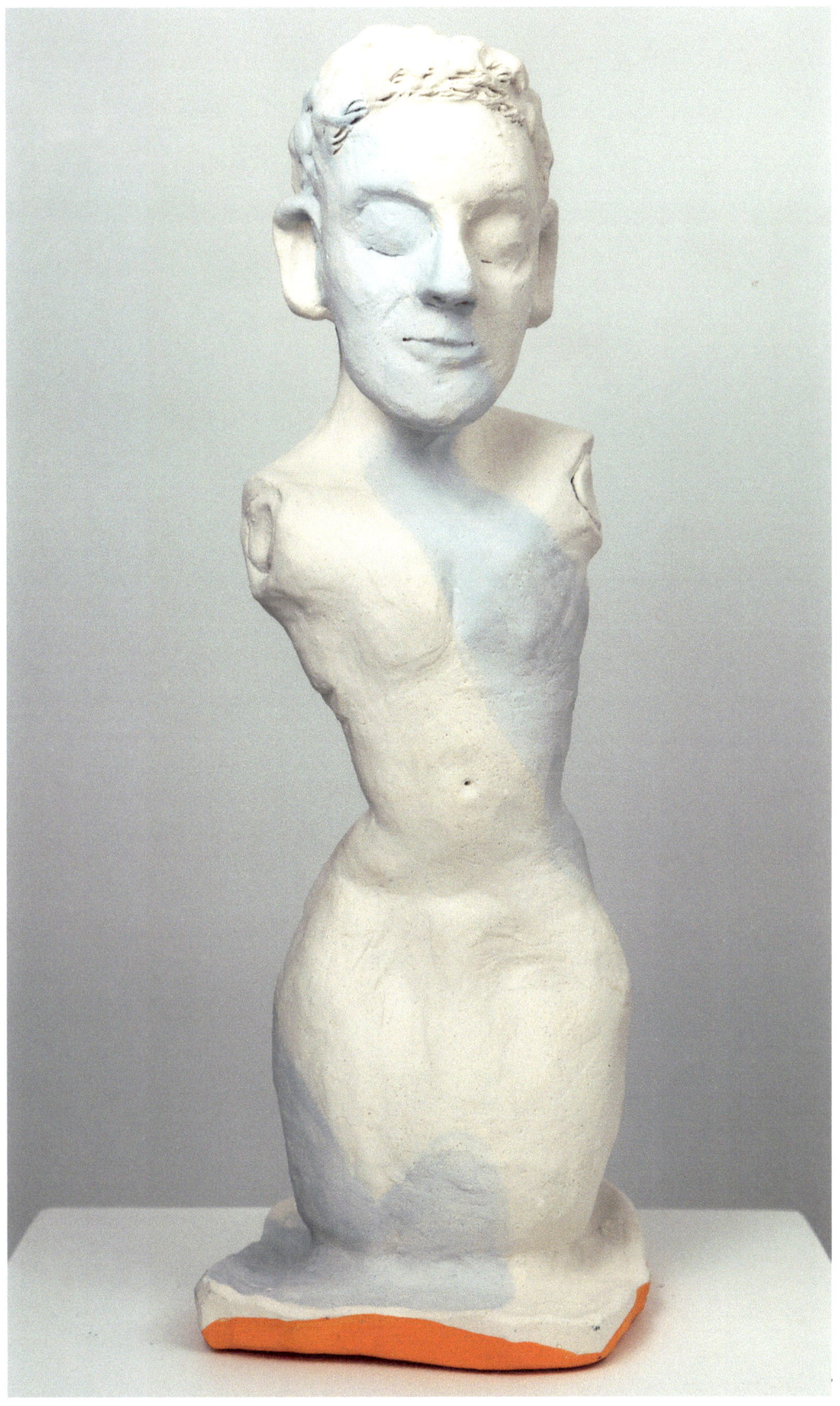

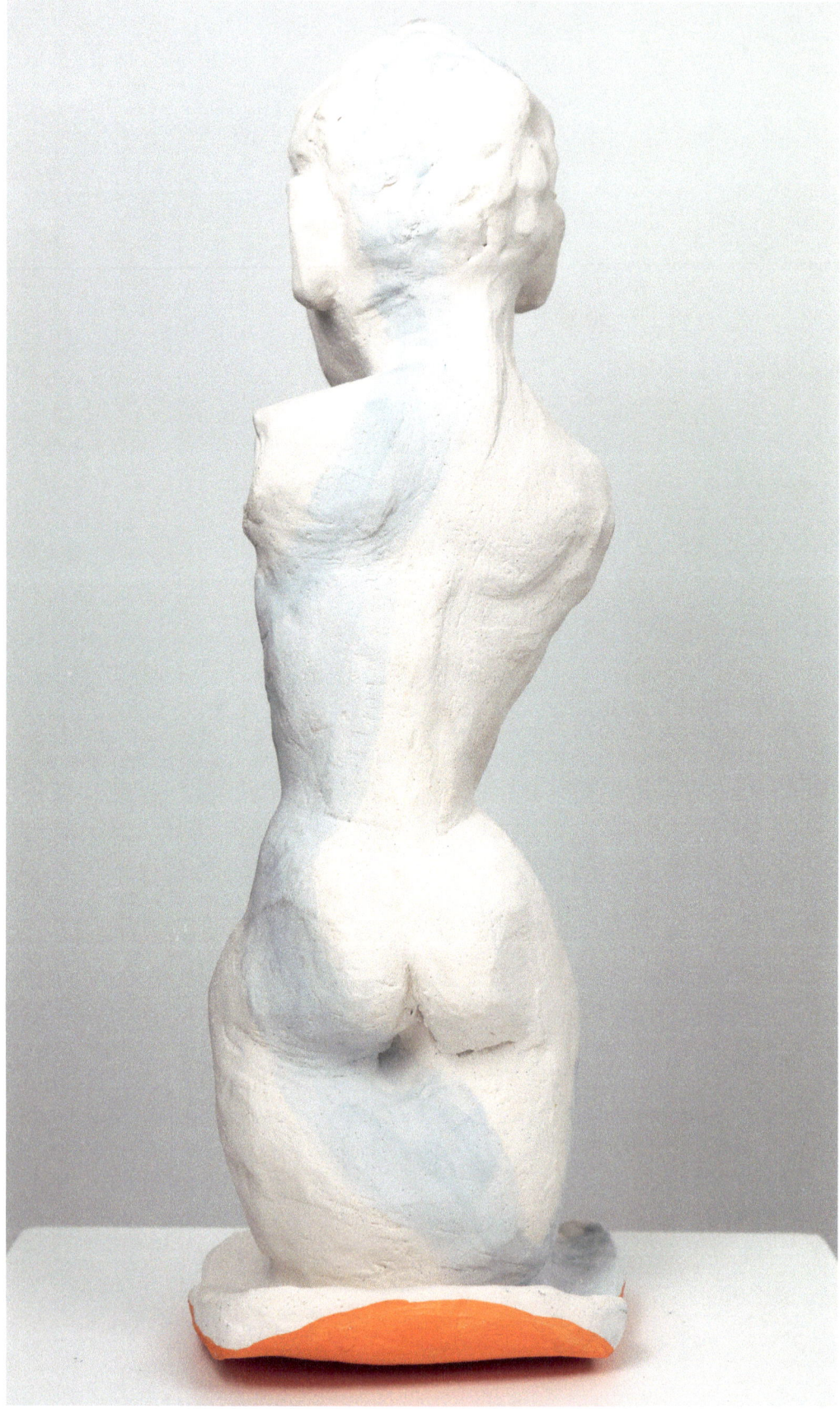

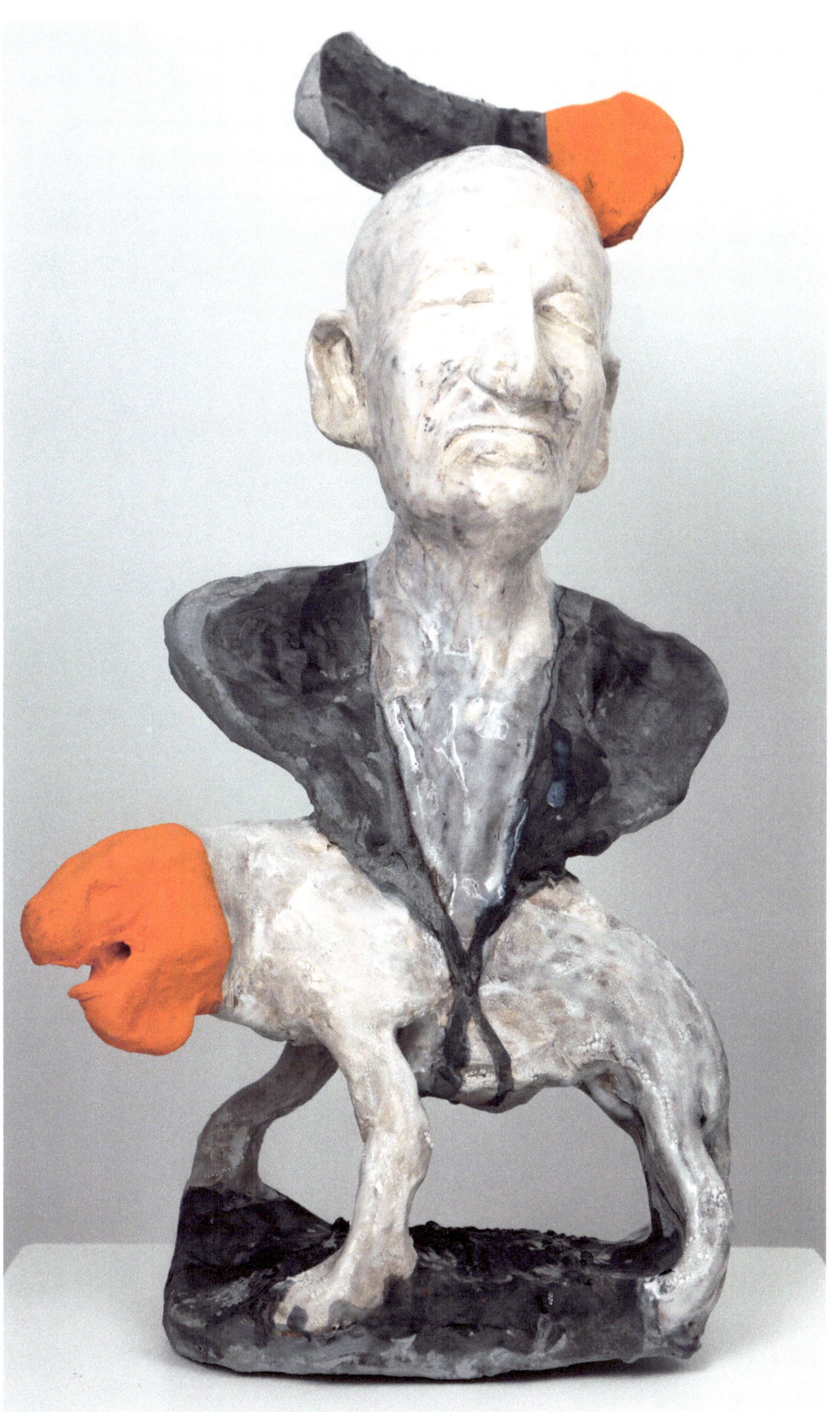

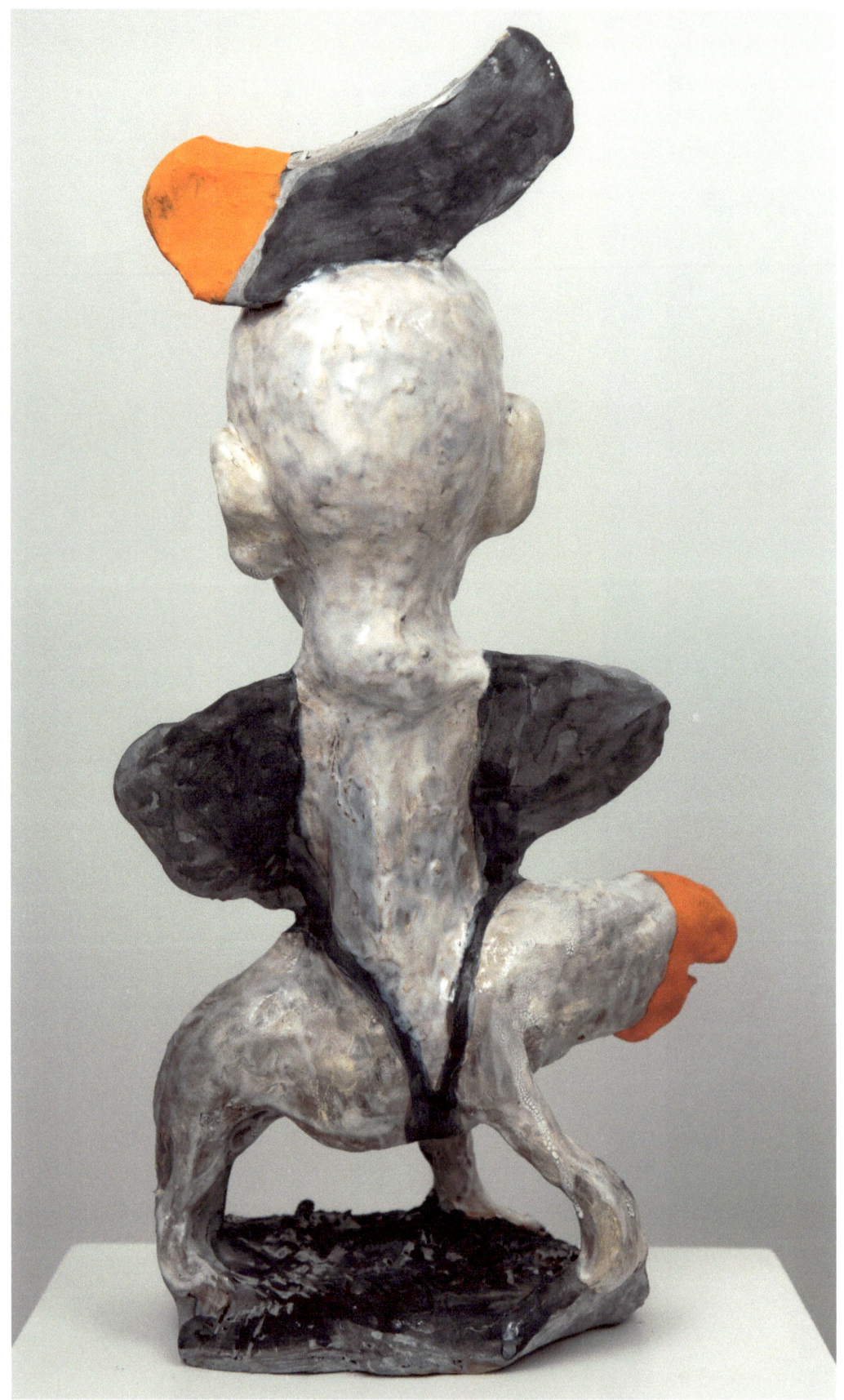

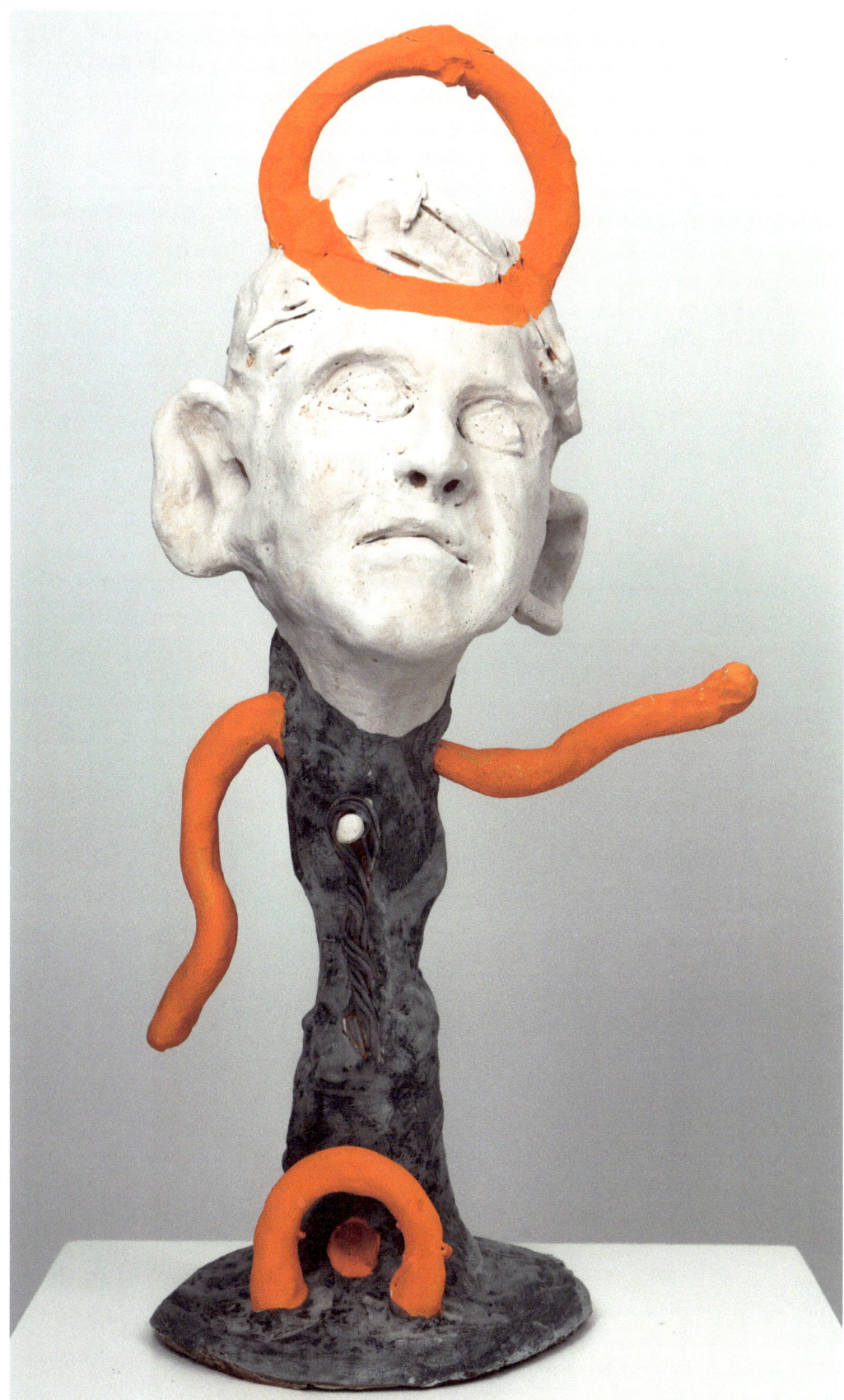

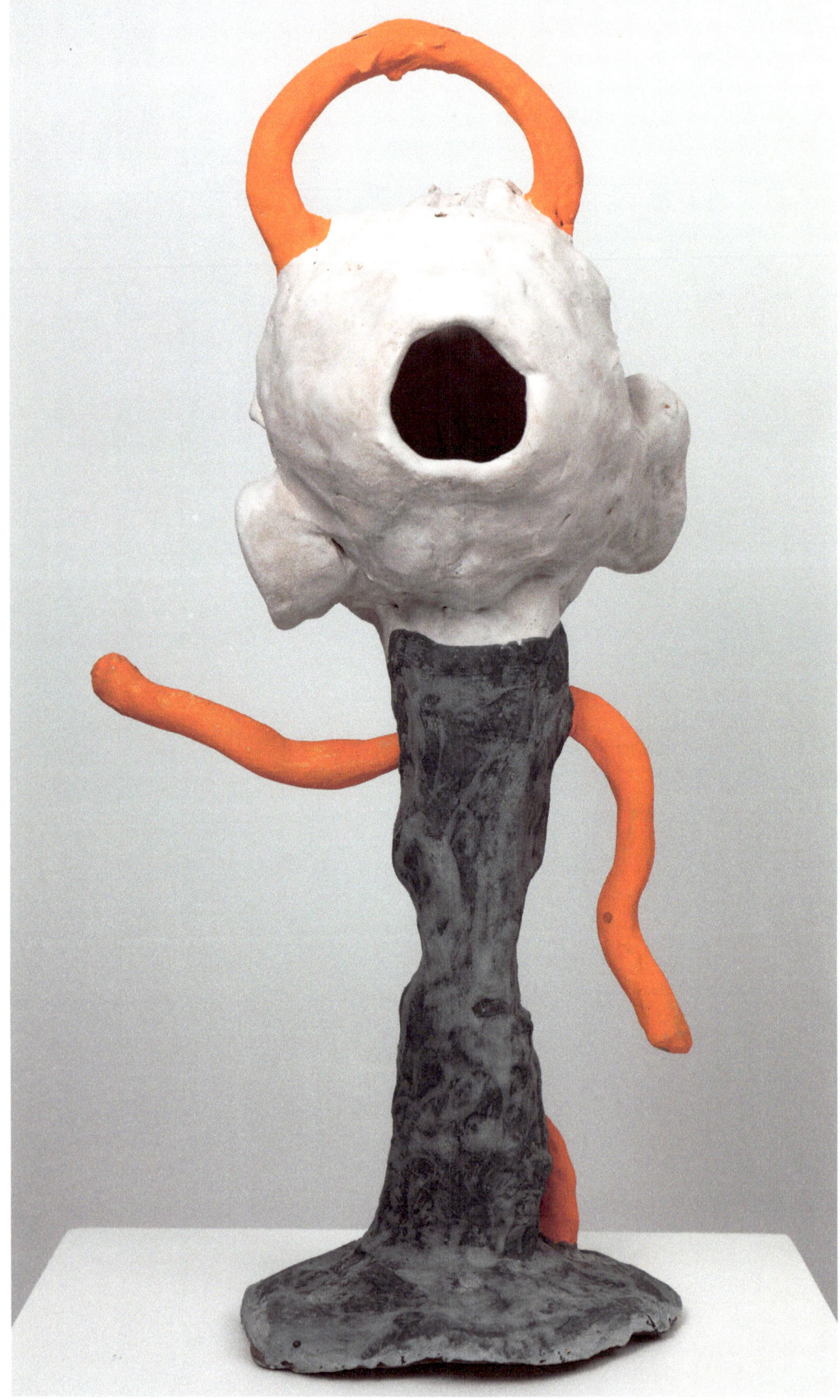

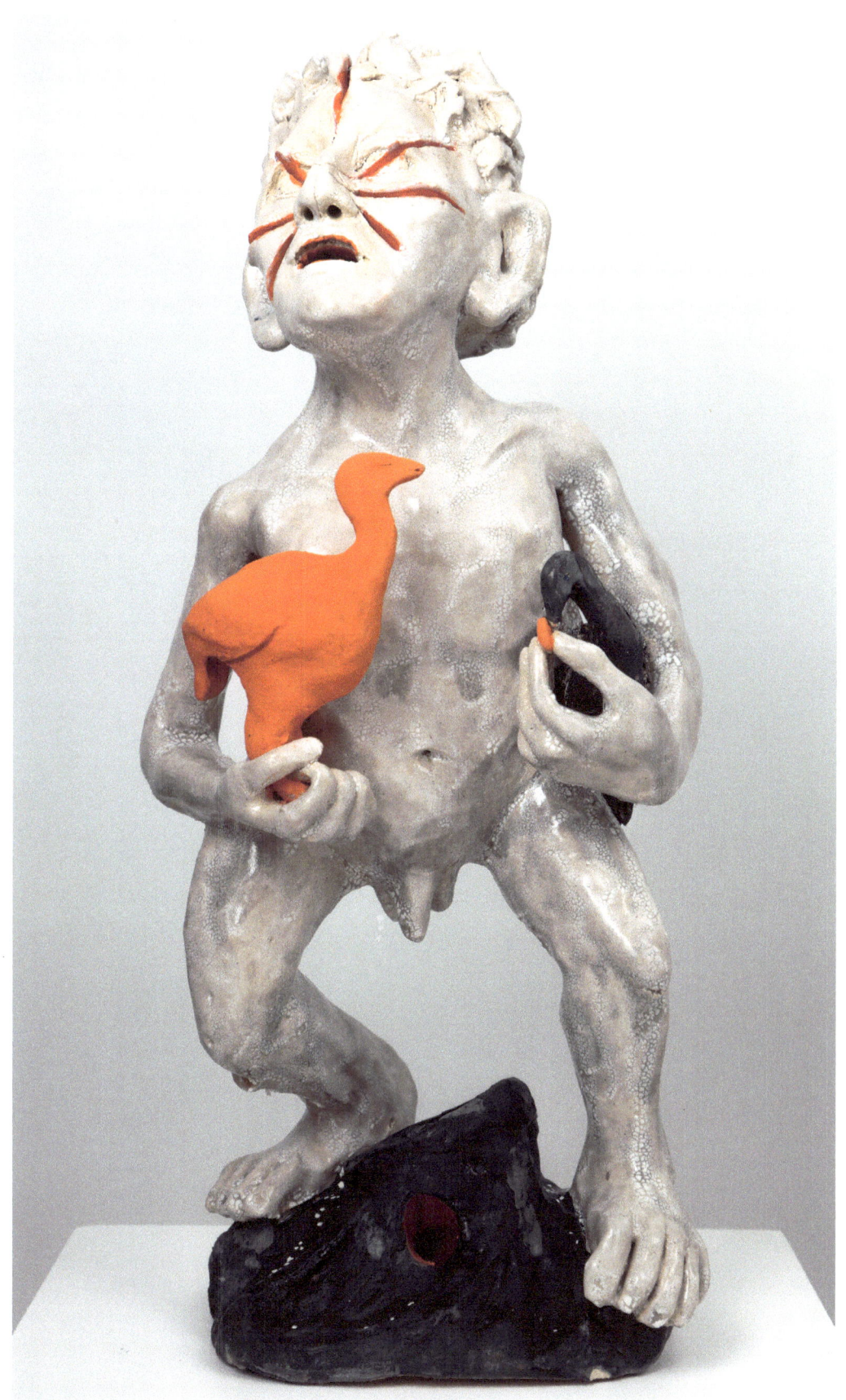

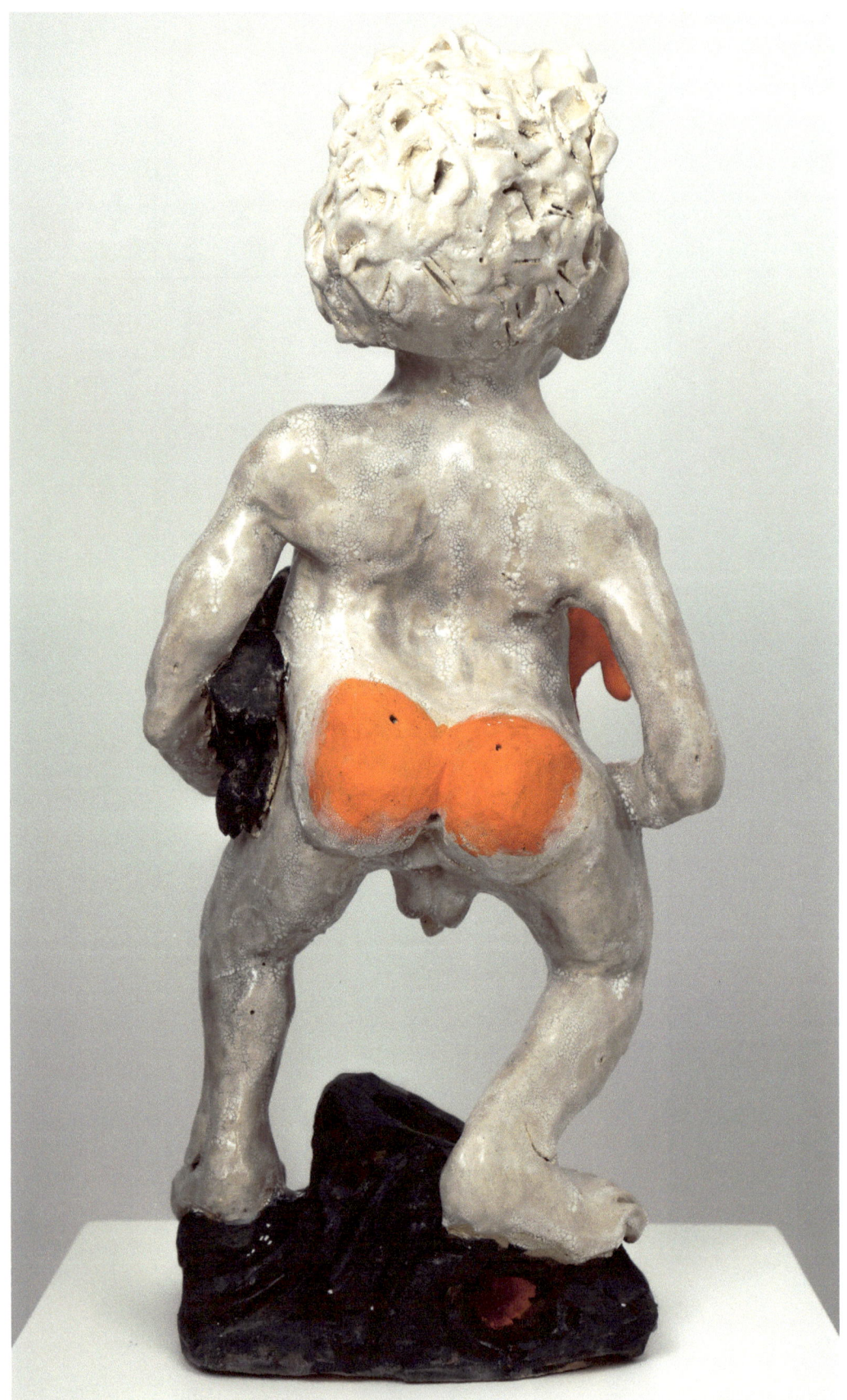

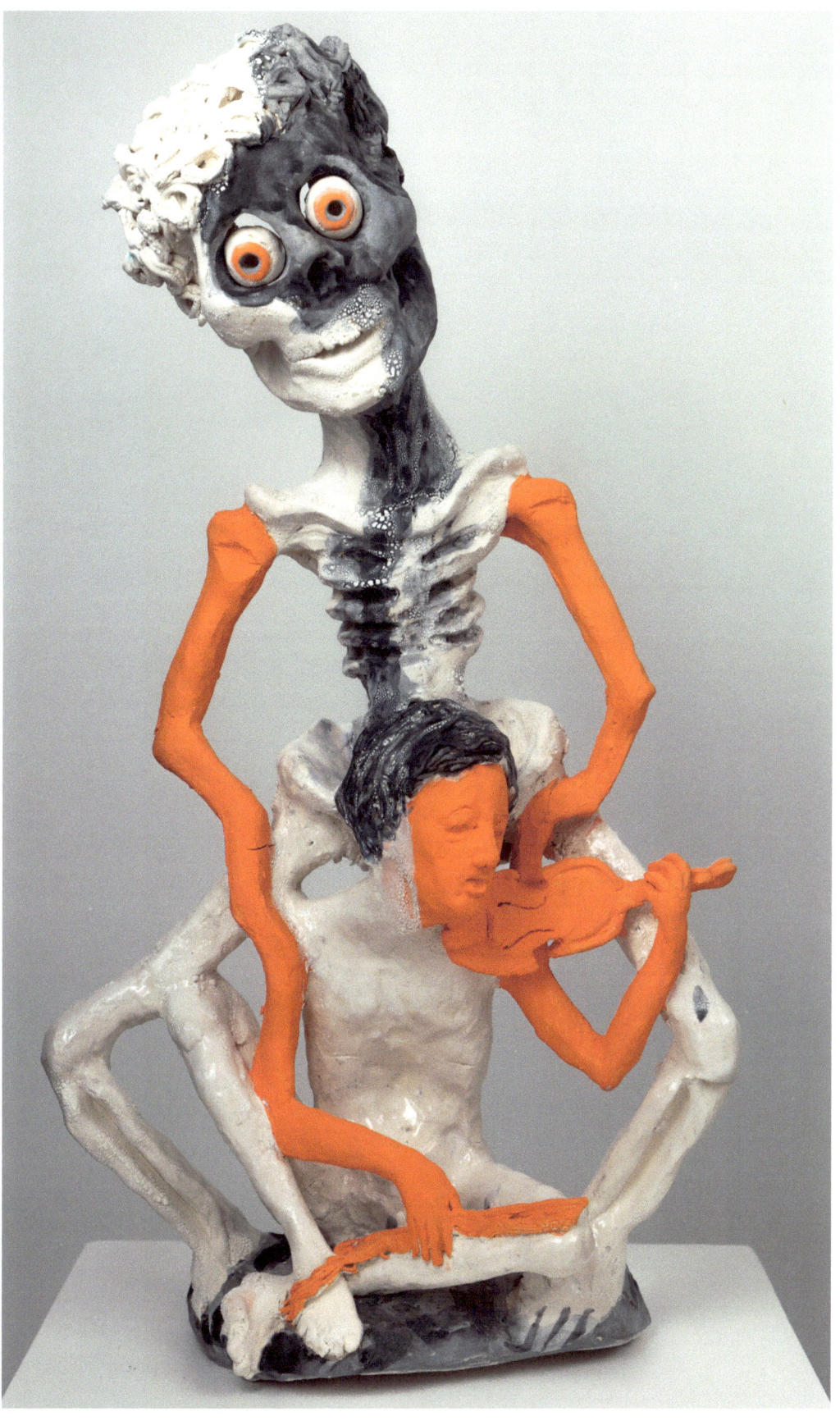

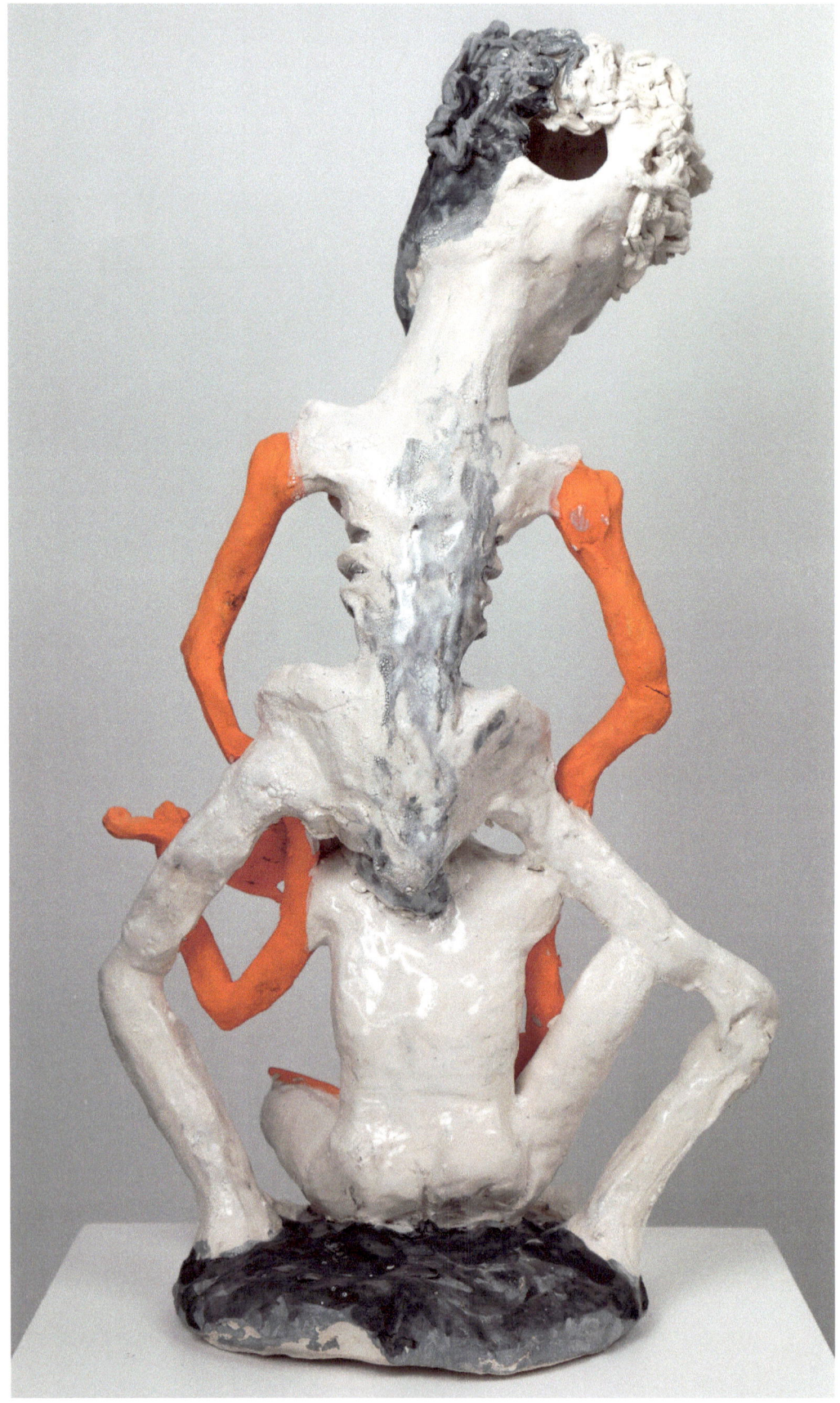

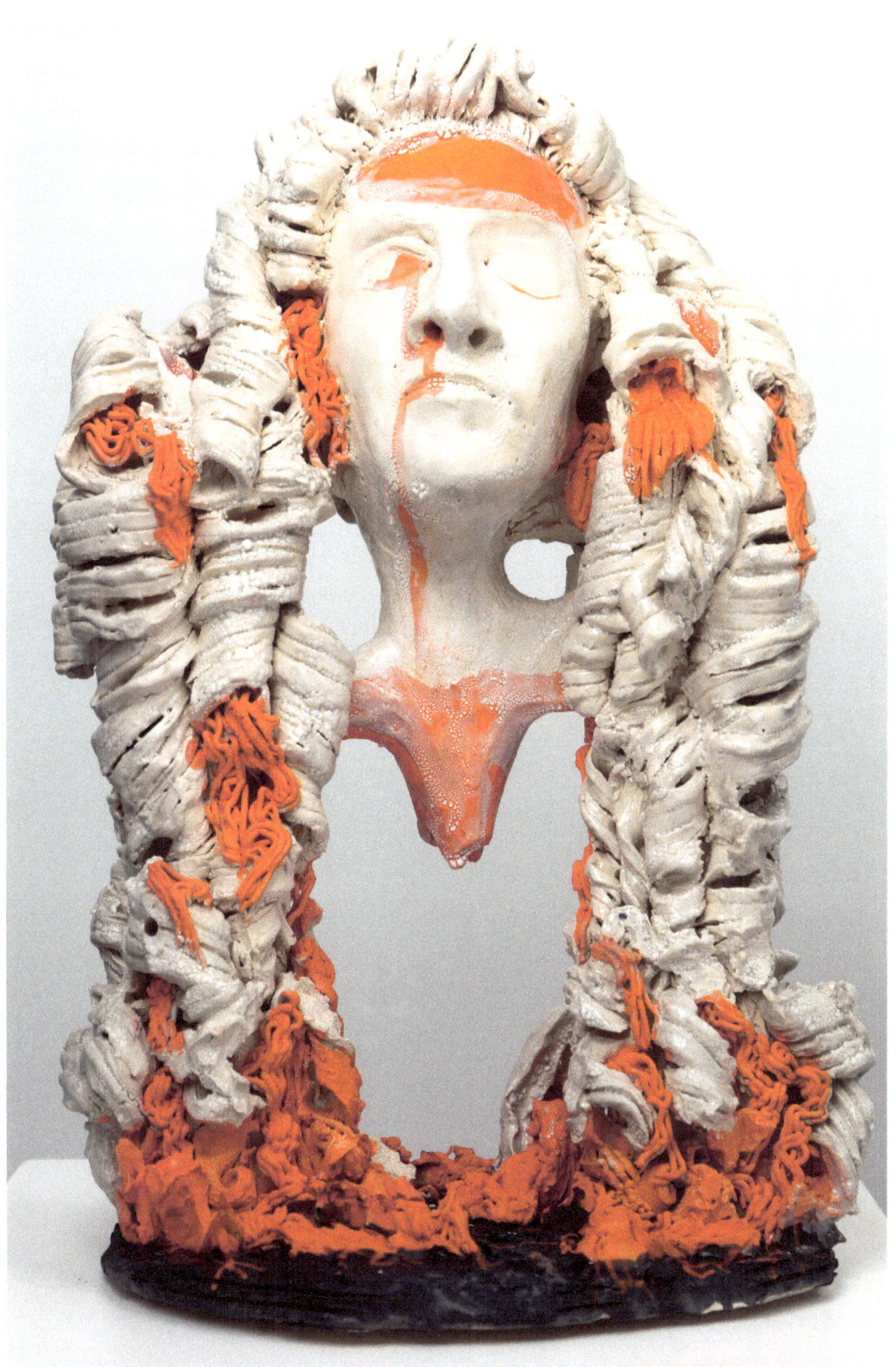

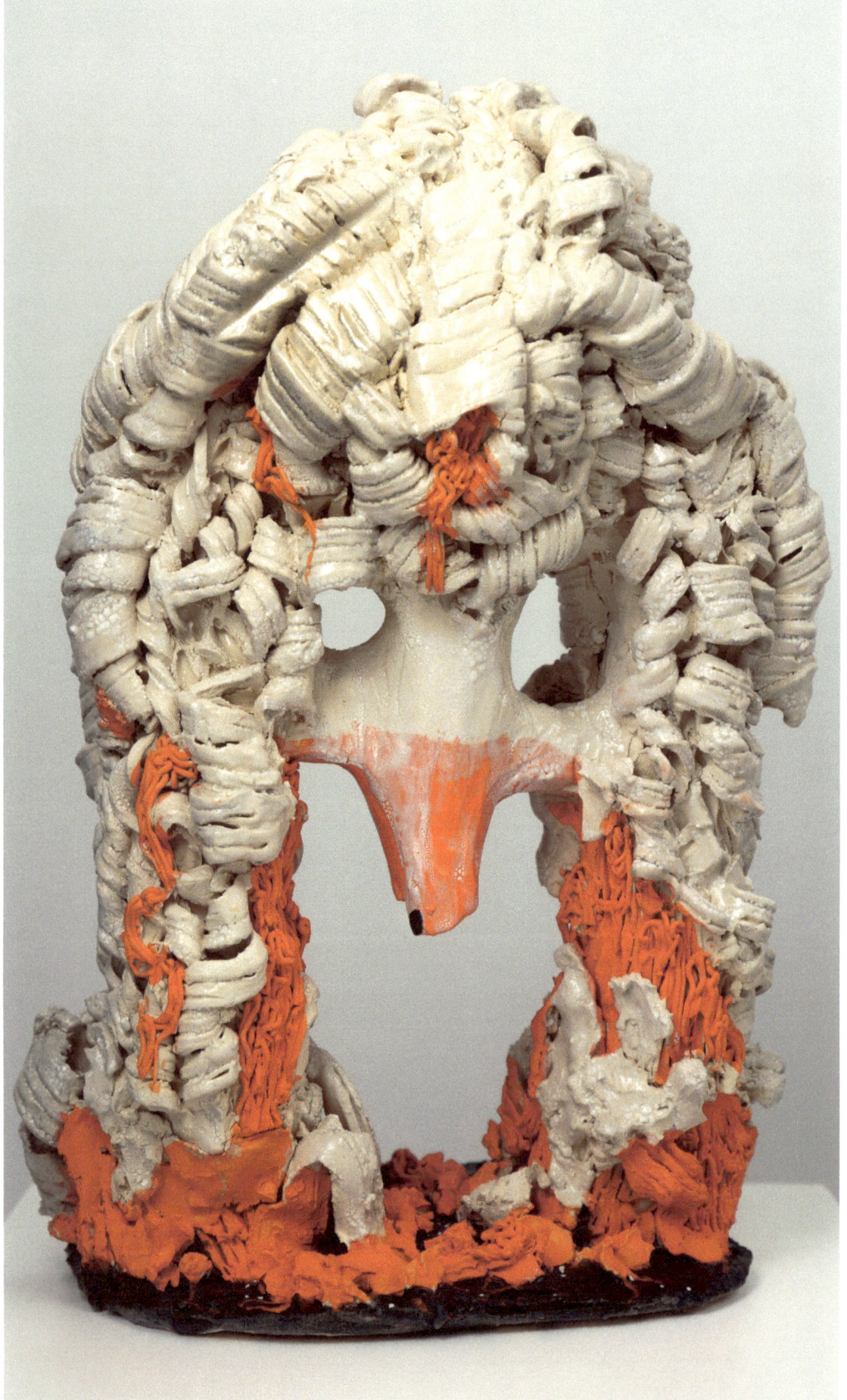

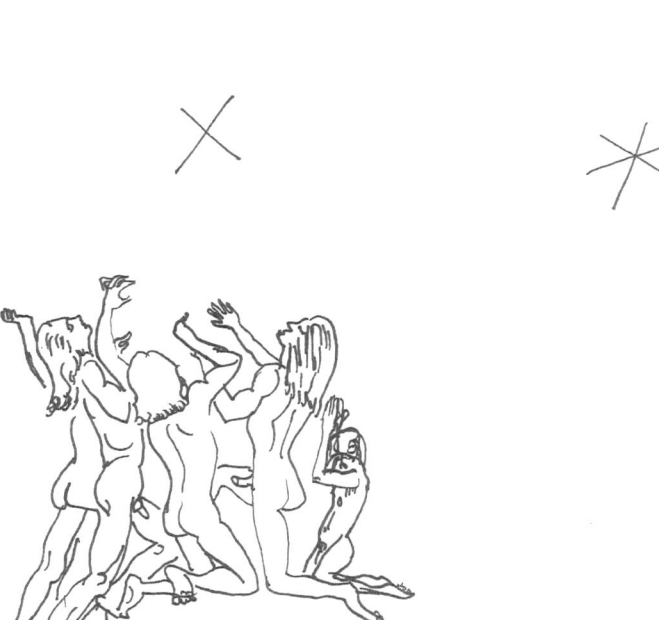

Works on Paper

Hyper Effigy

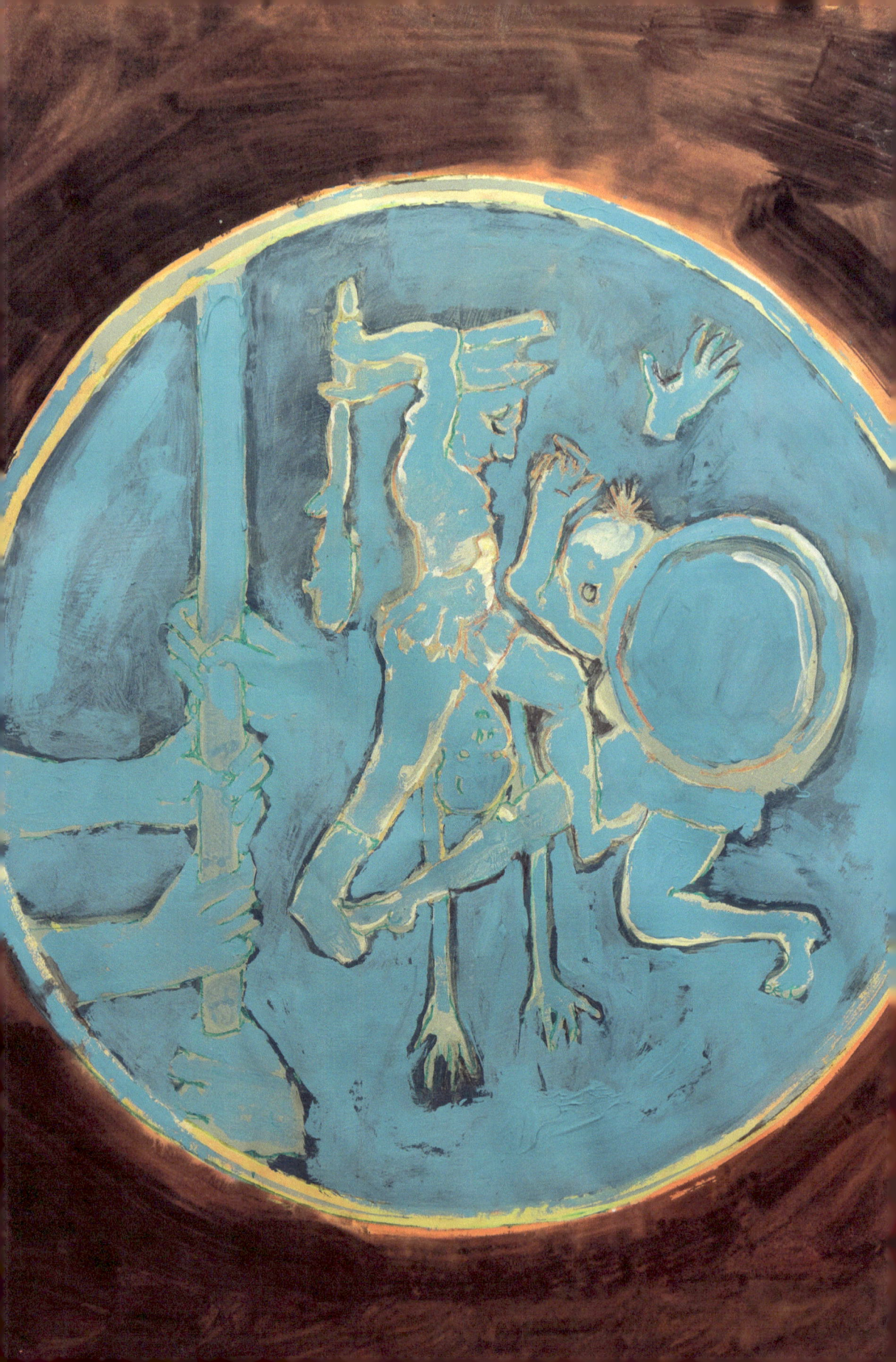

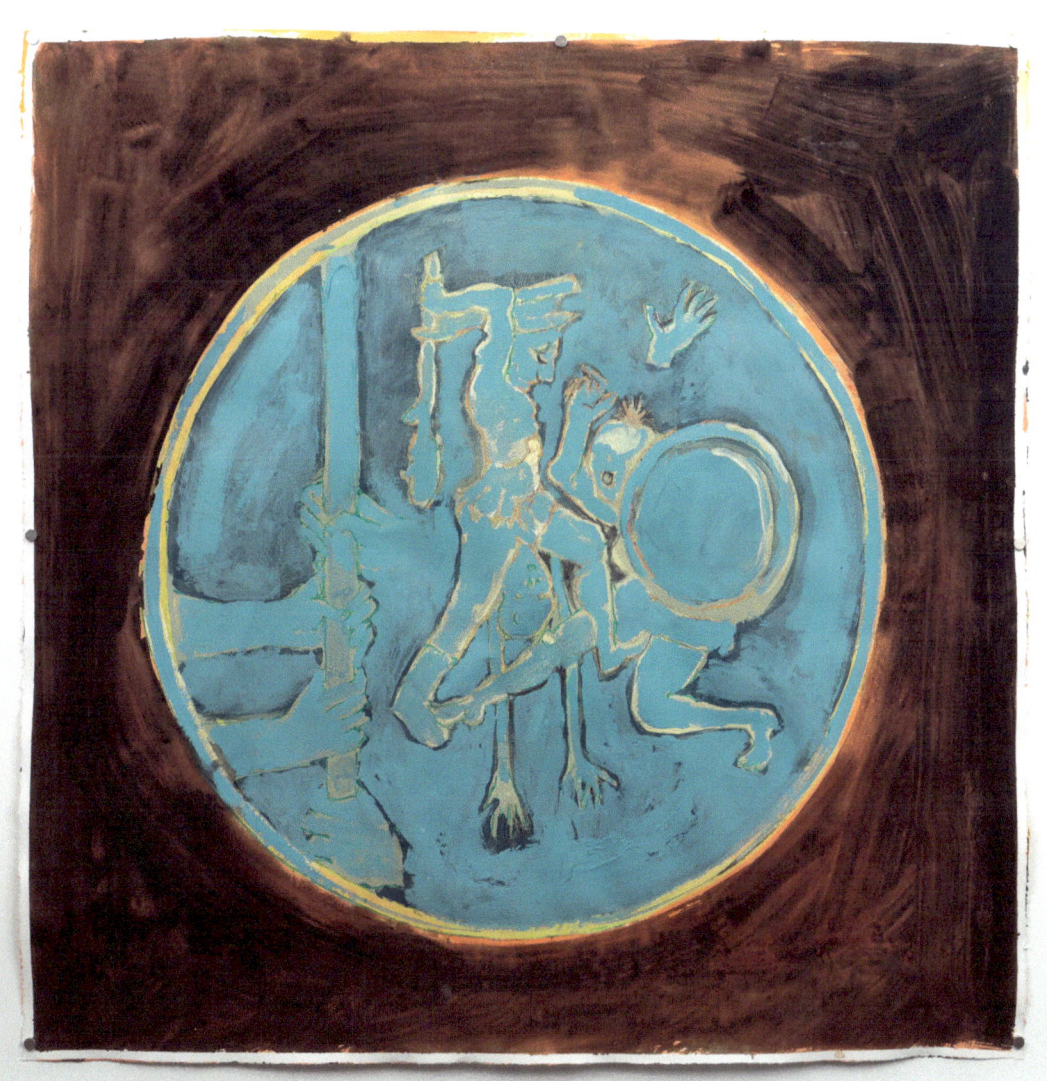

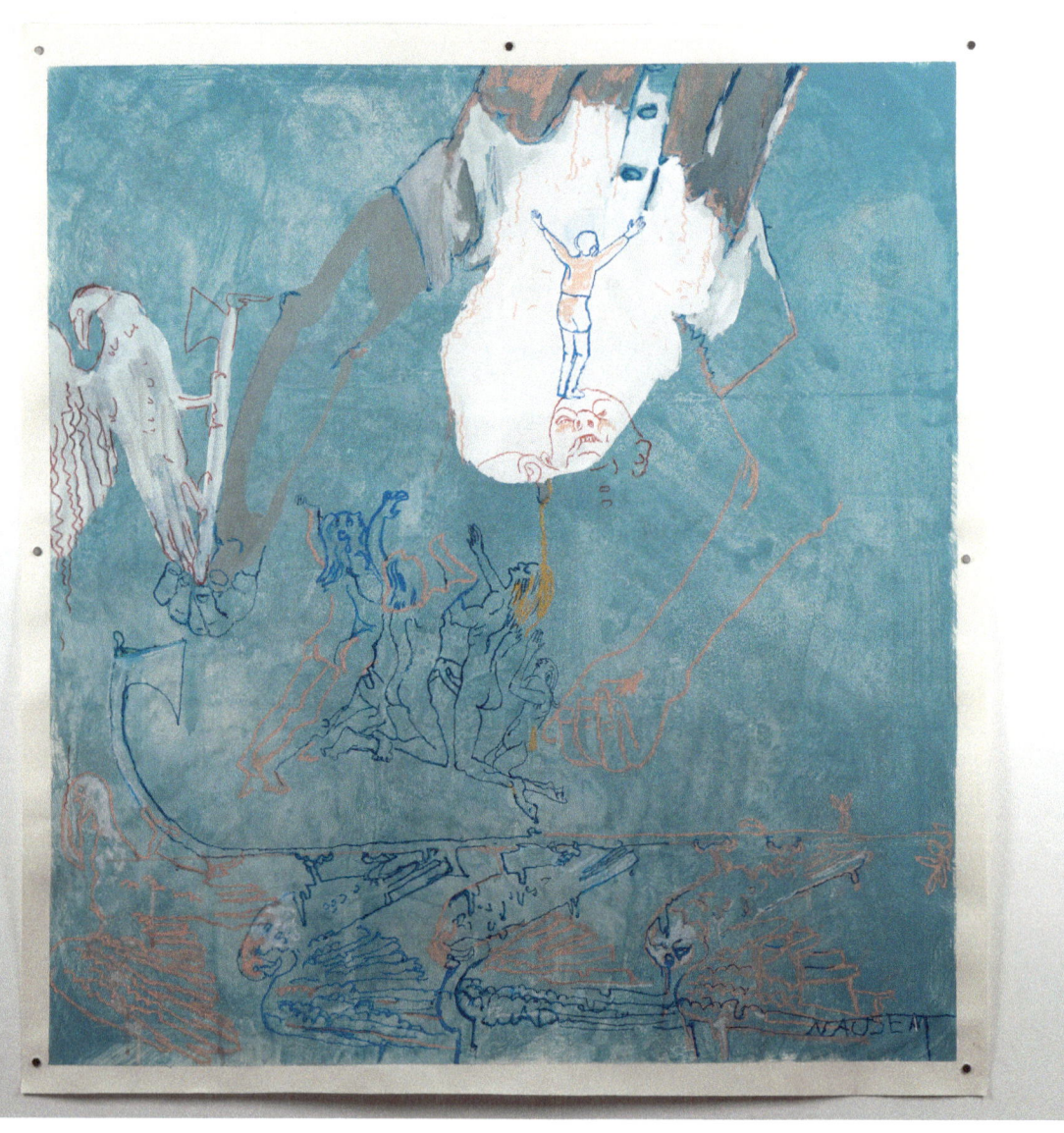

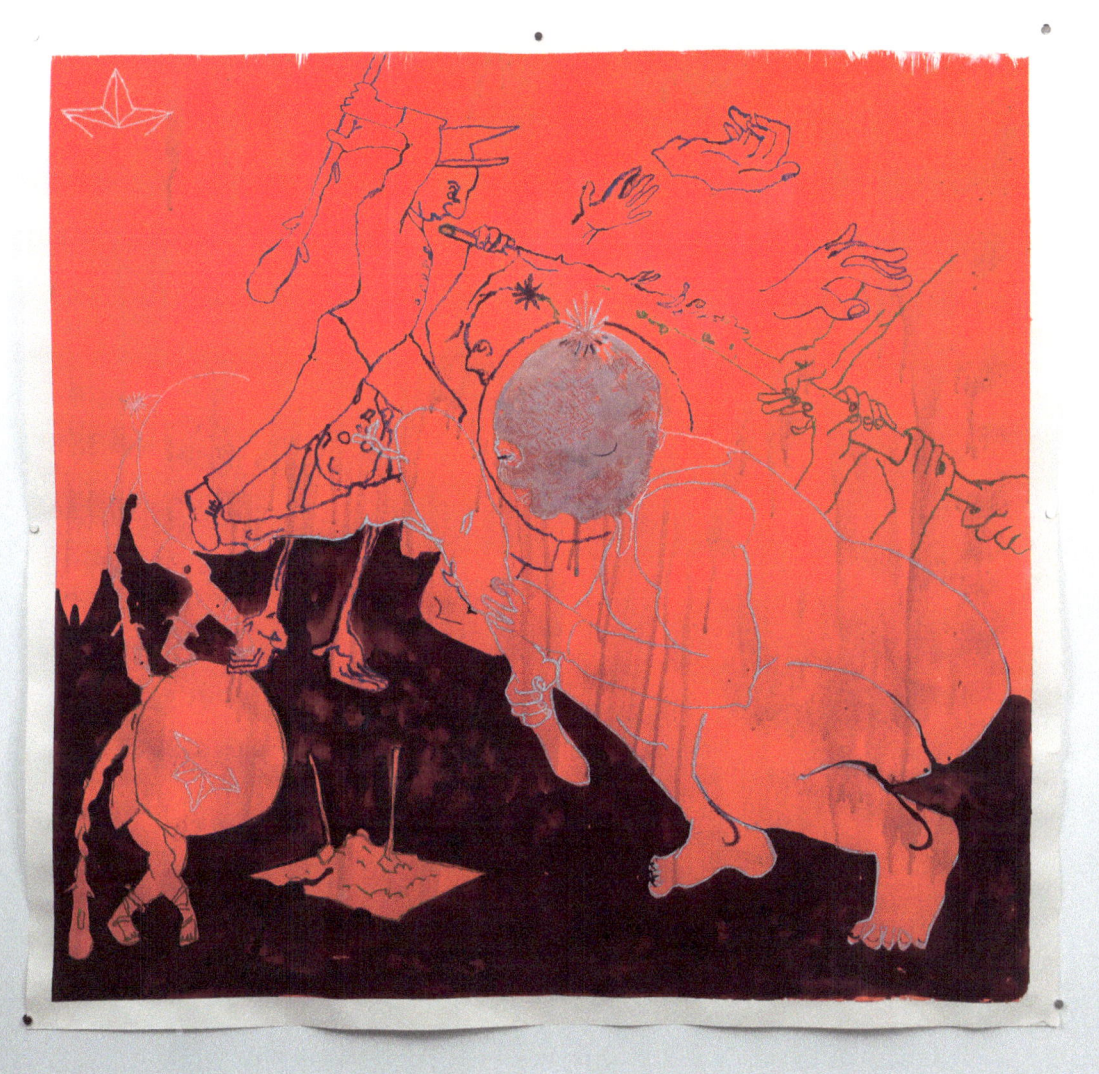

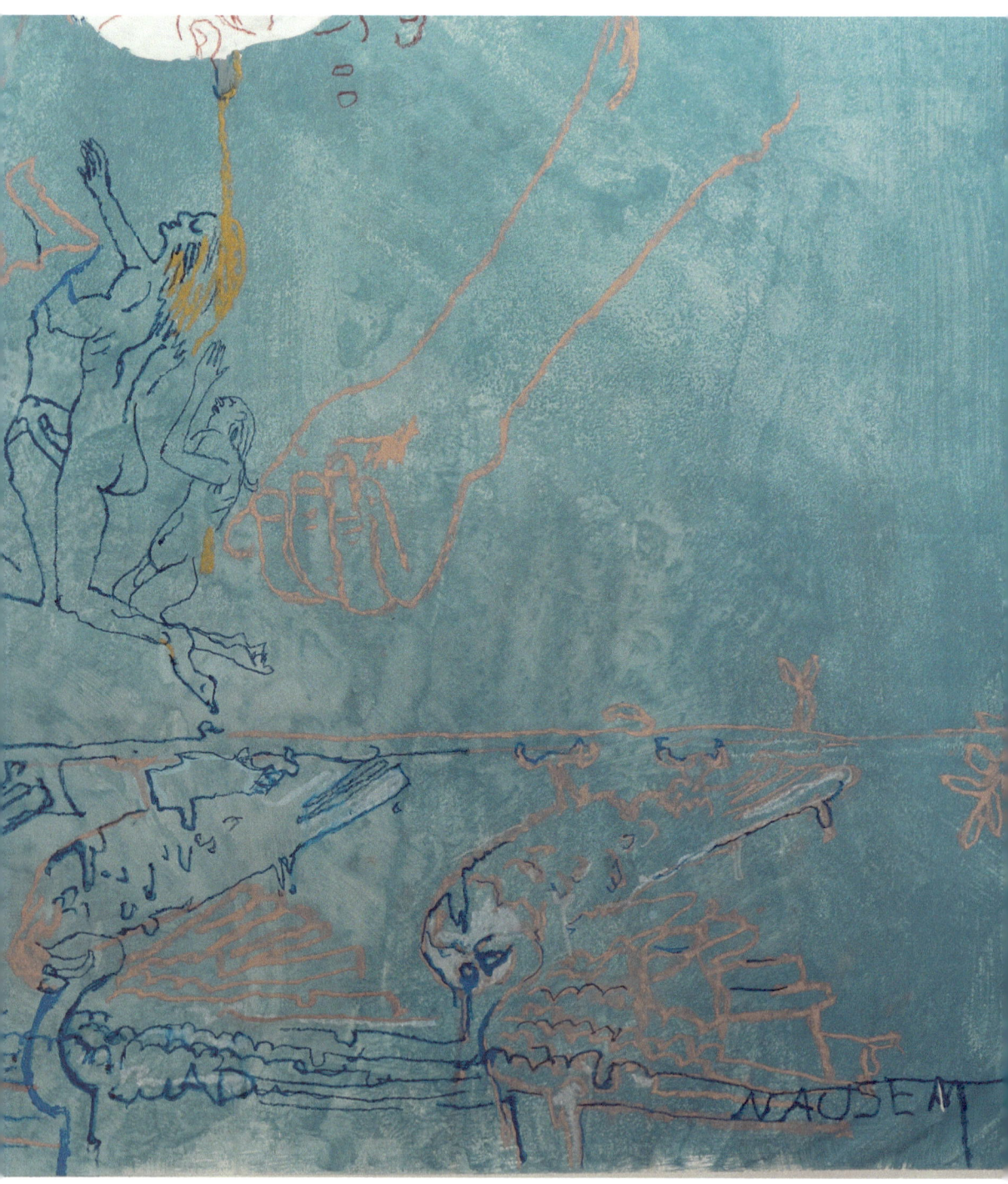

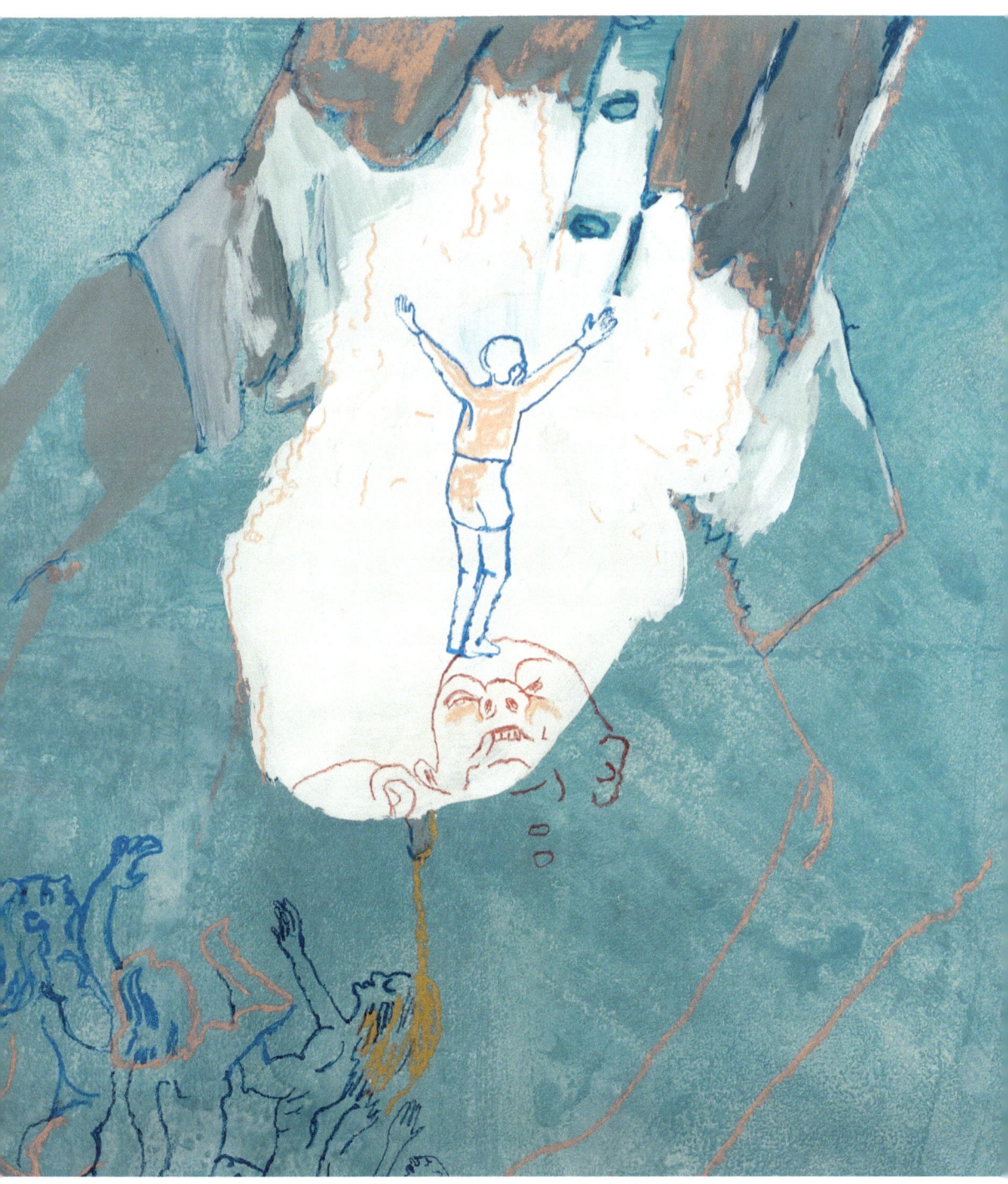

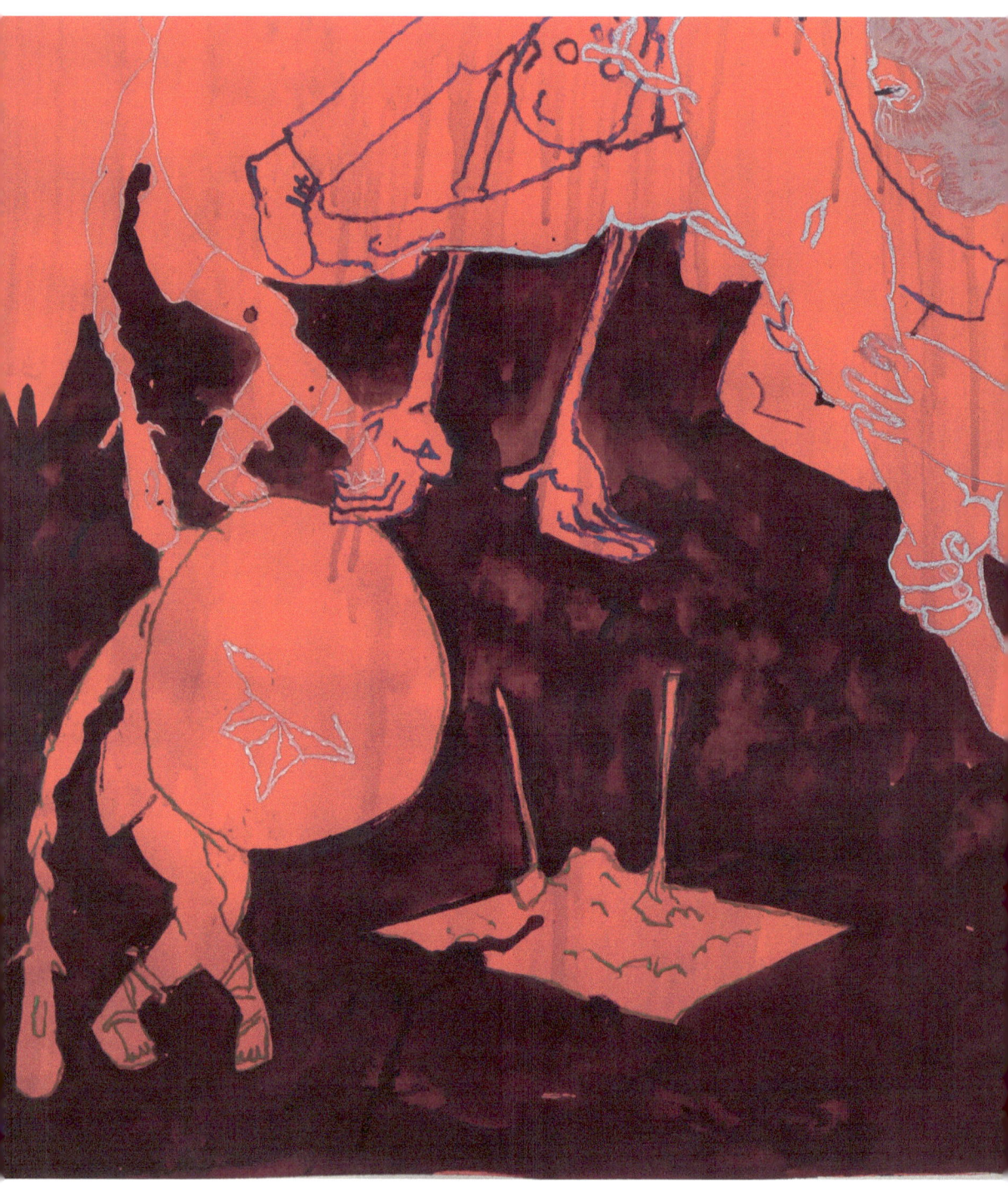

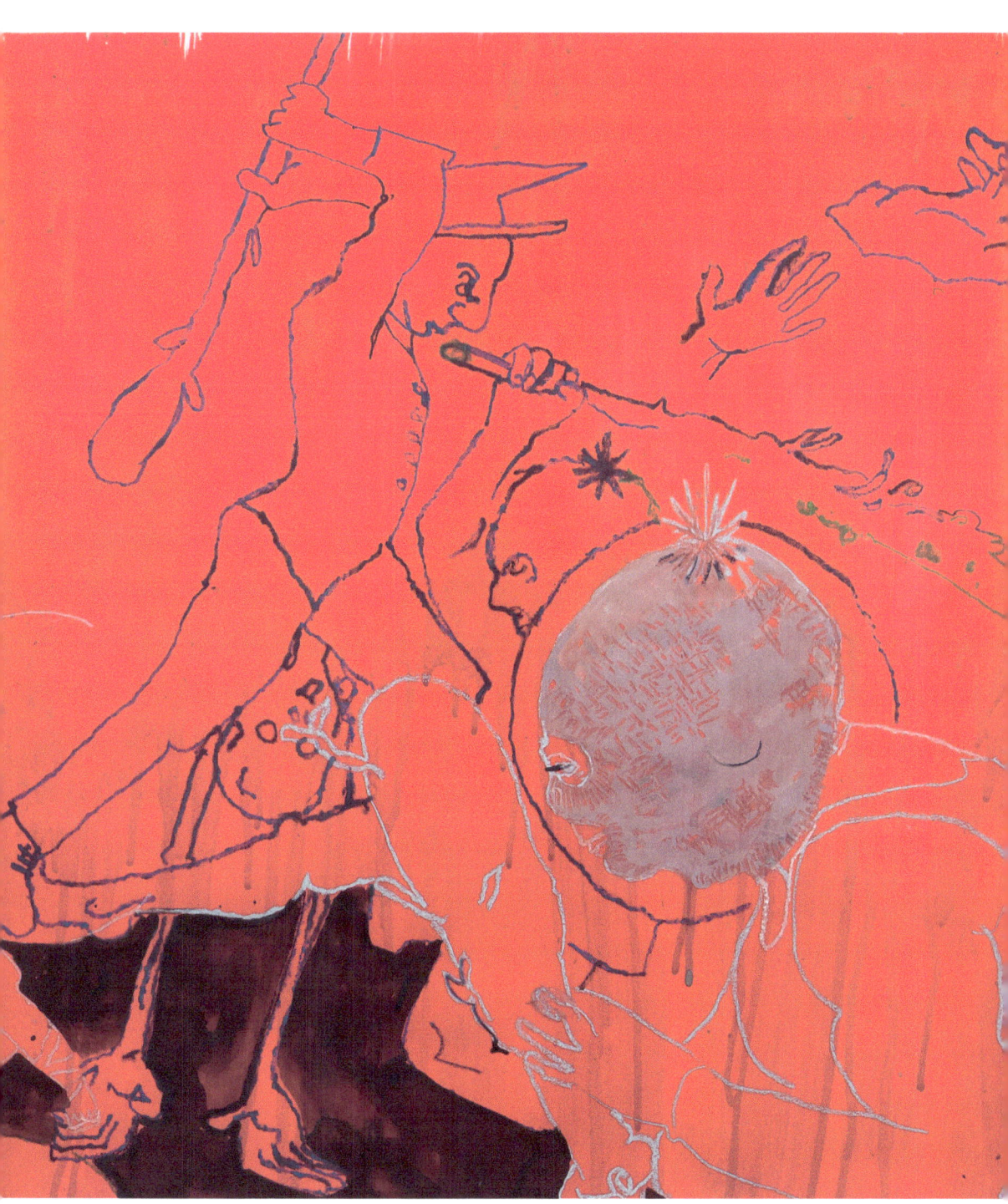

Ersatz Fighting Unit

Hyper Effigy

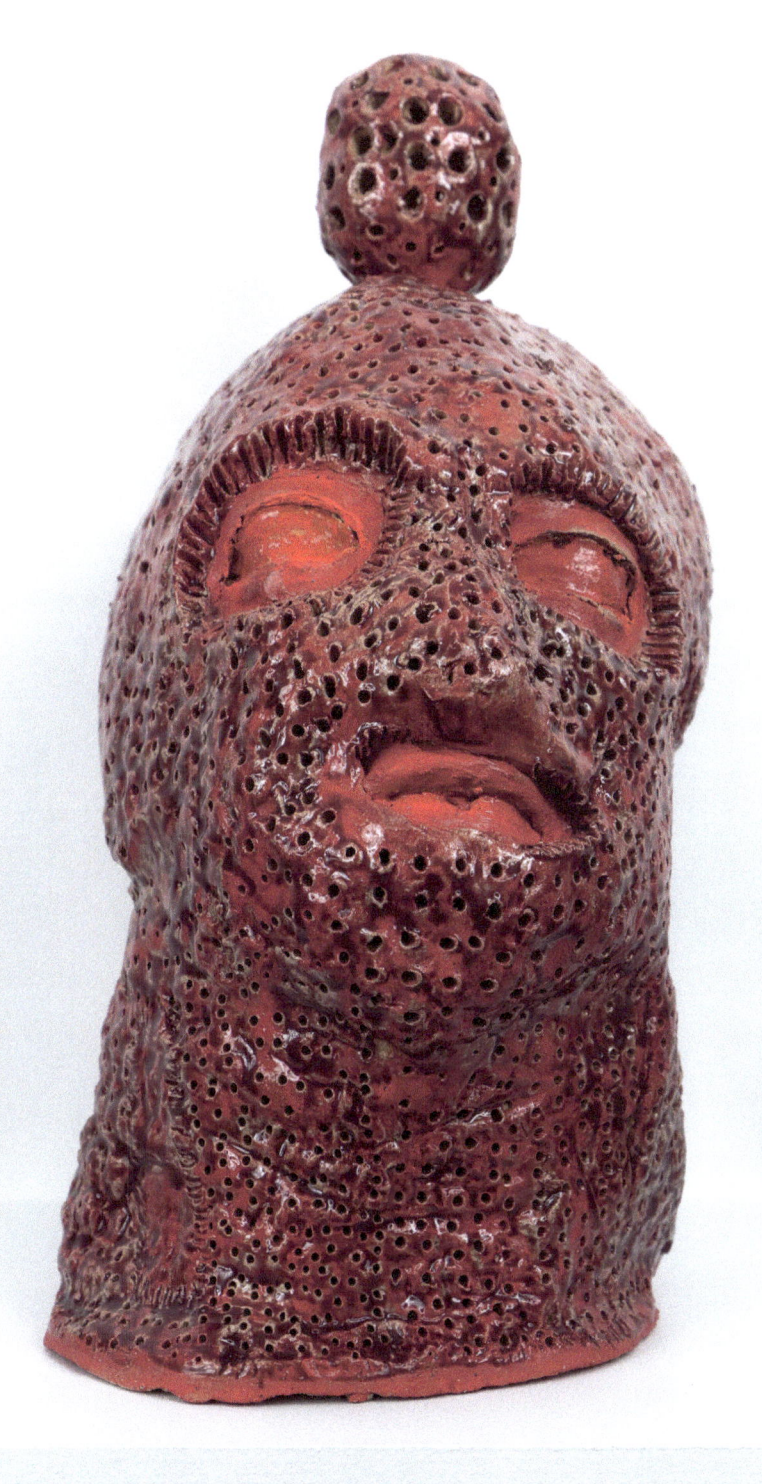

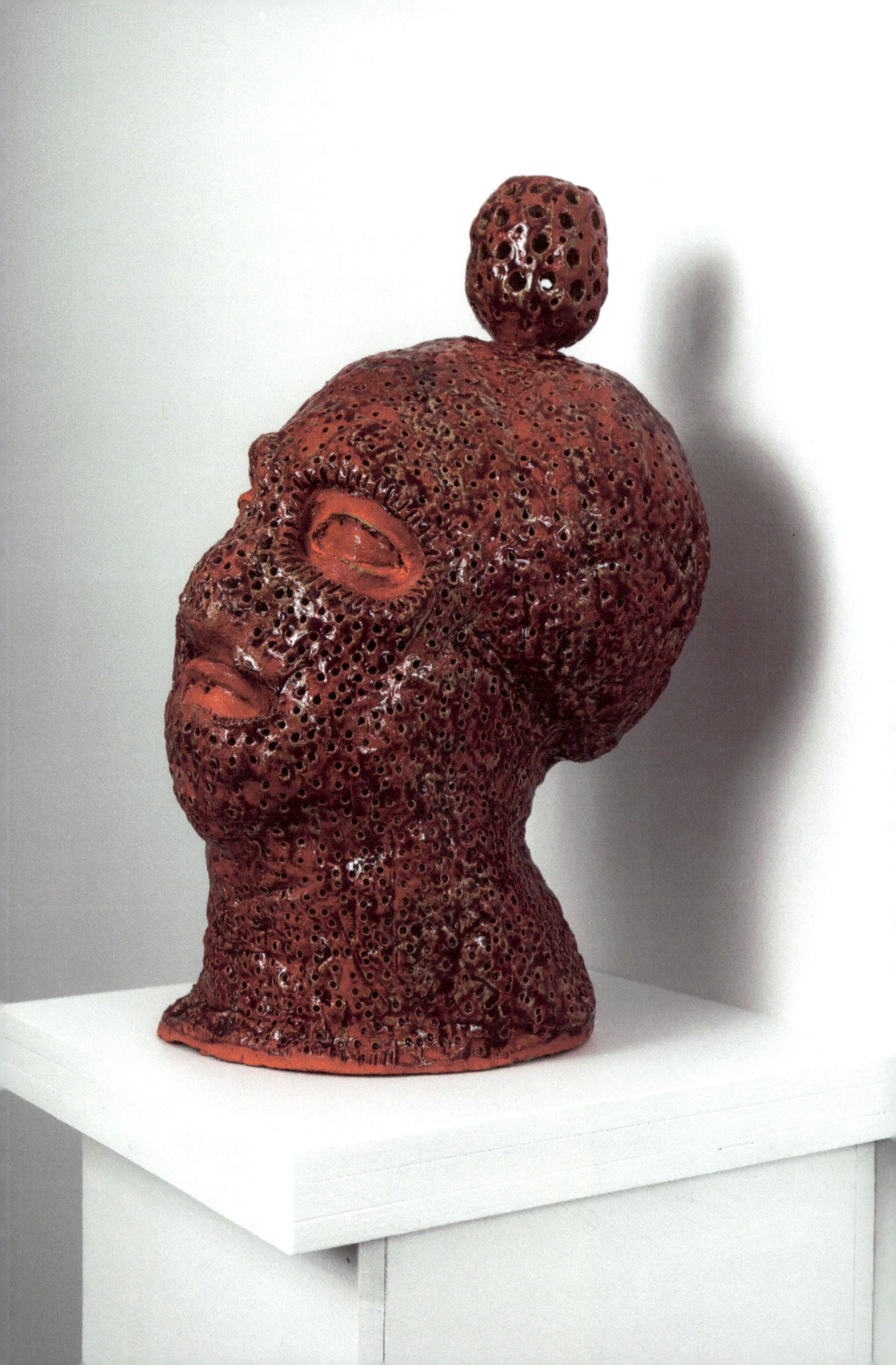

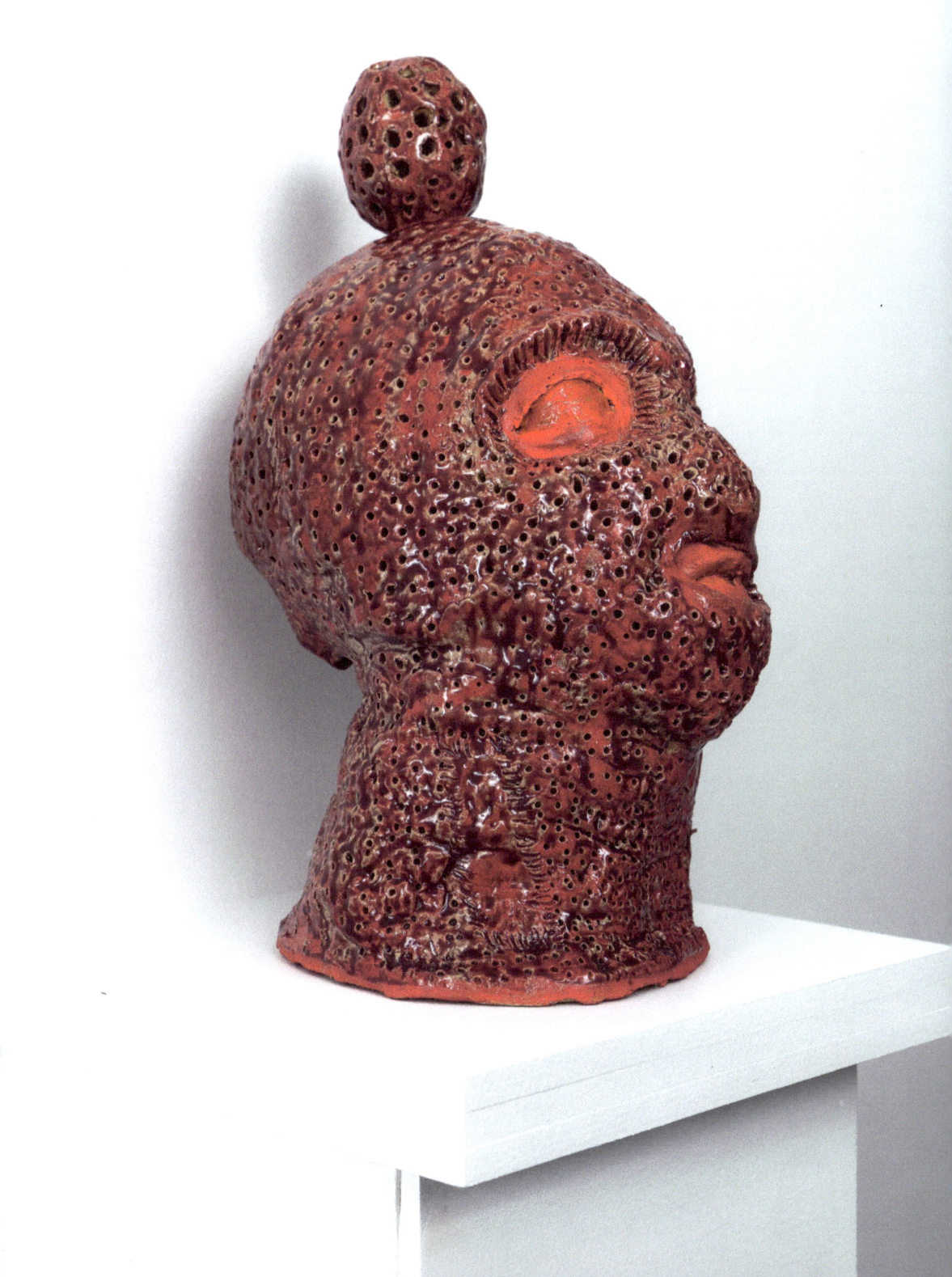

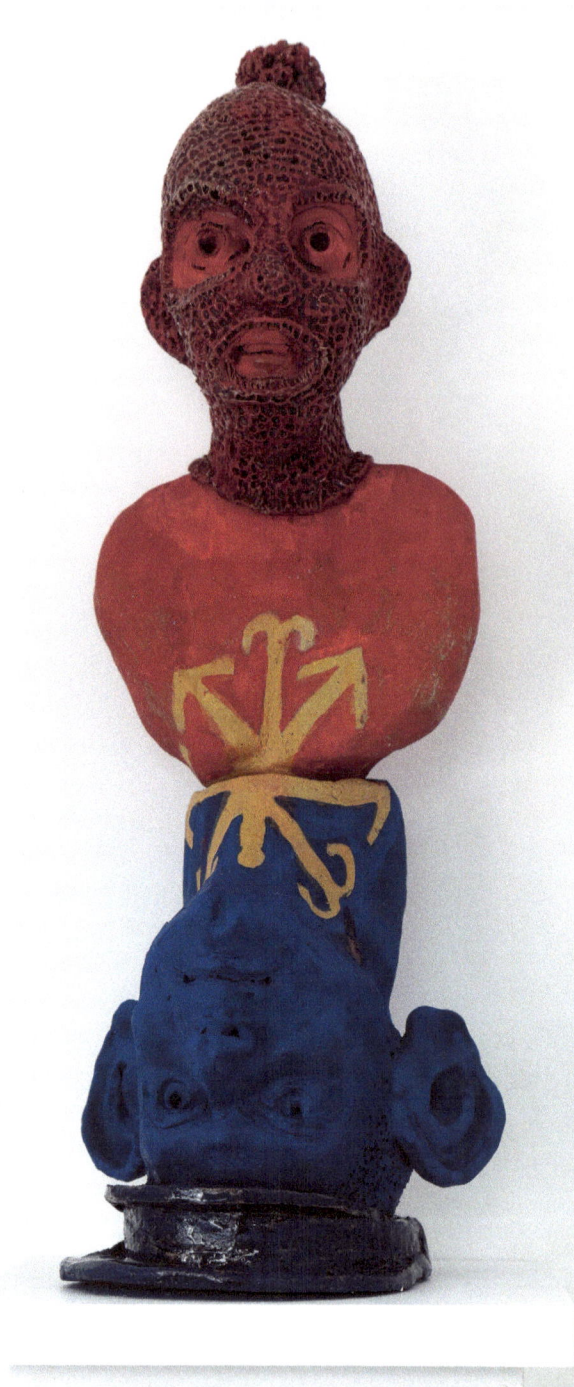

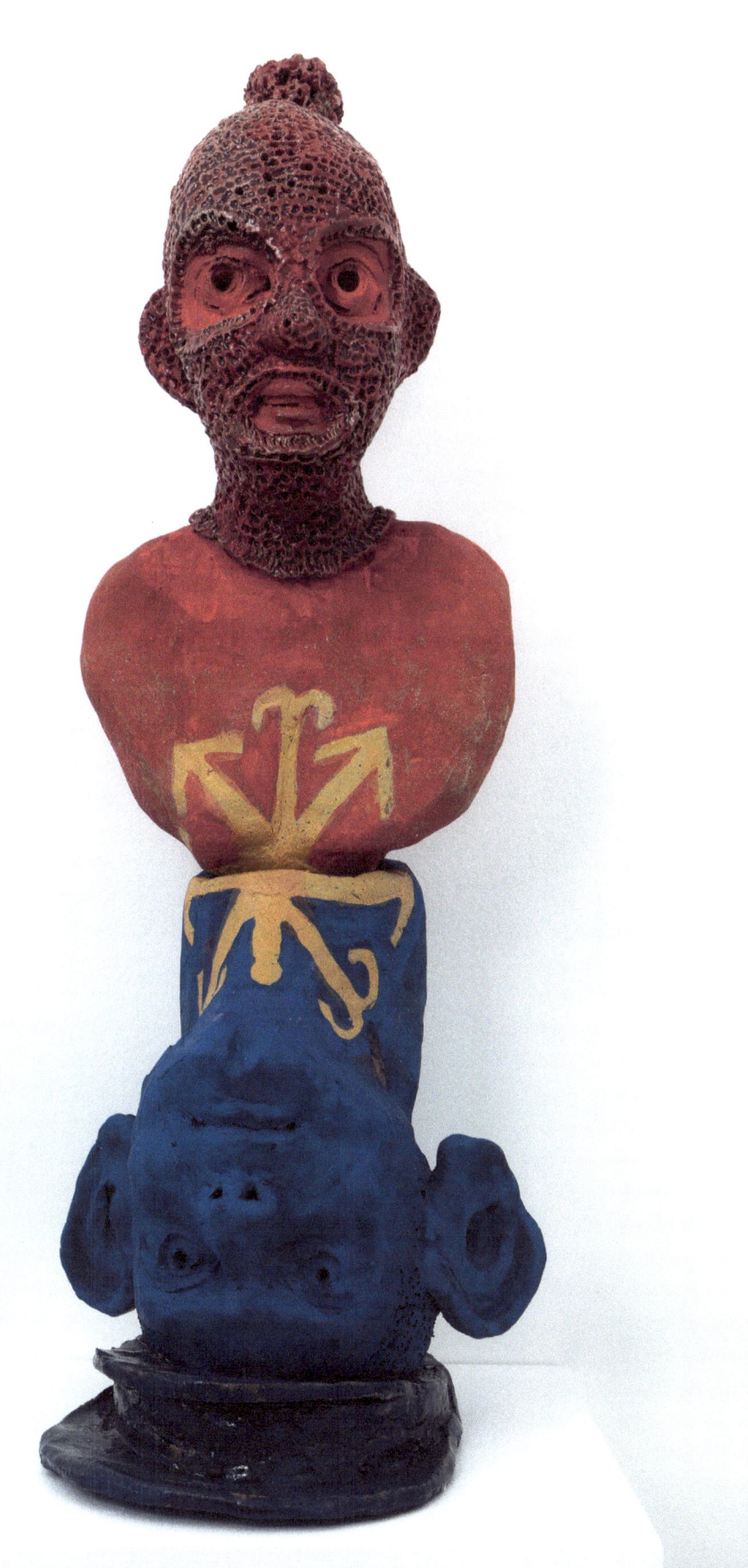

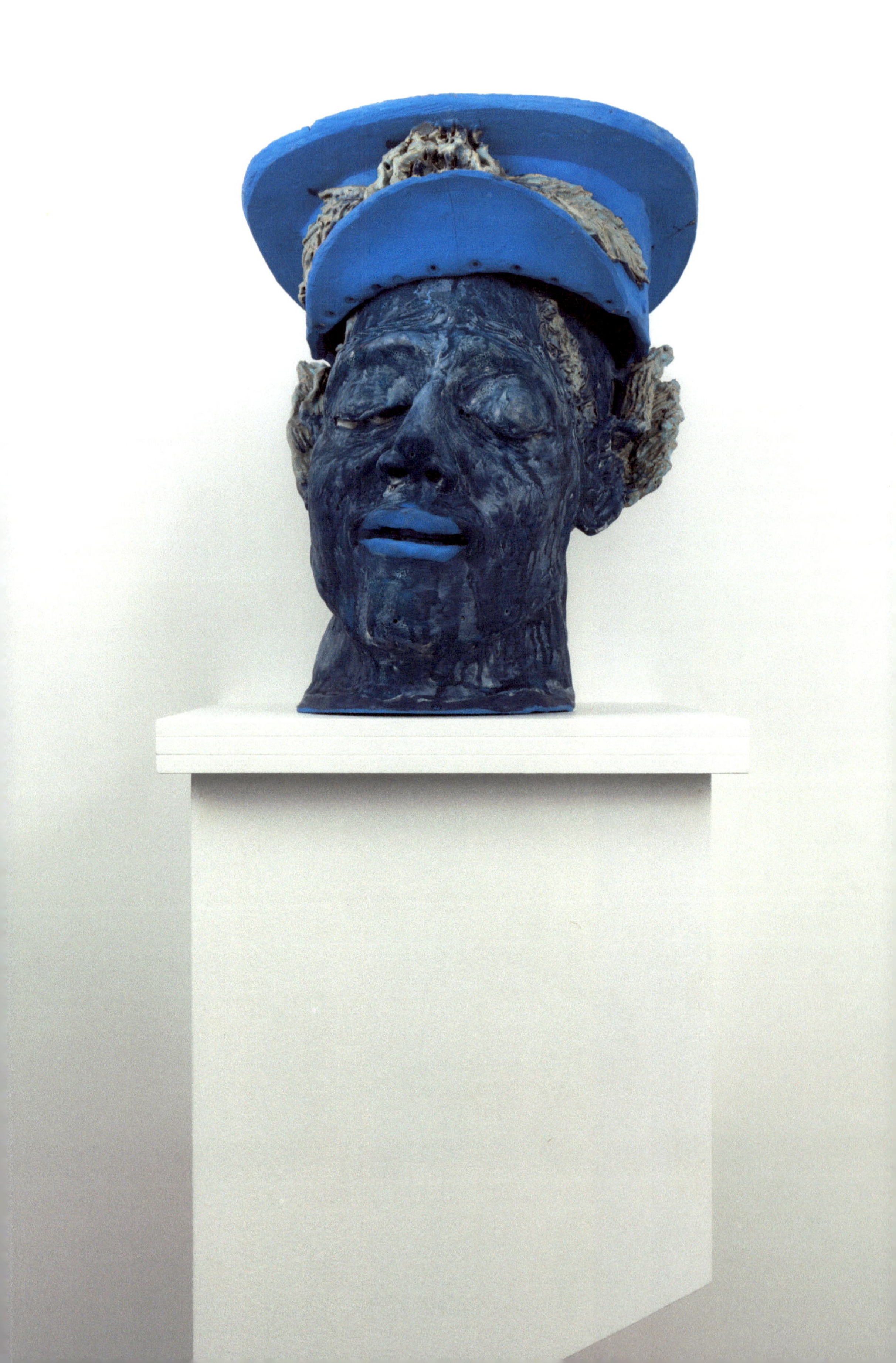

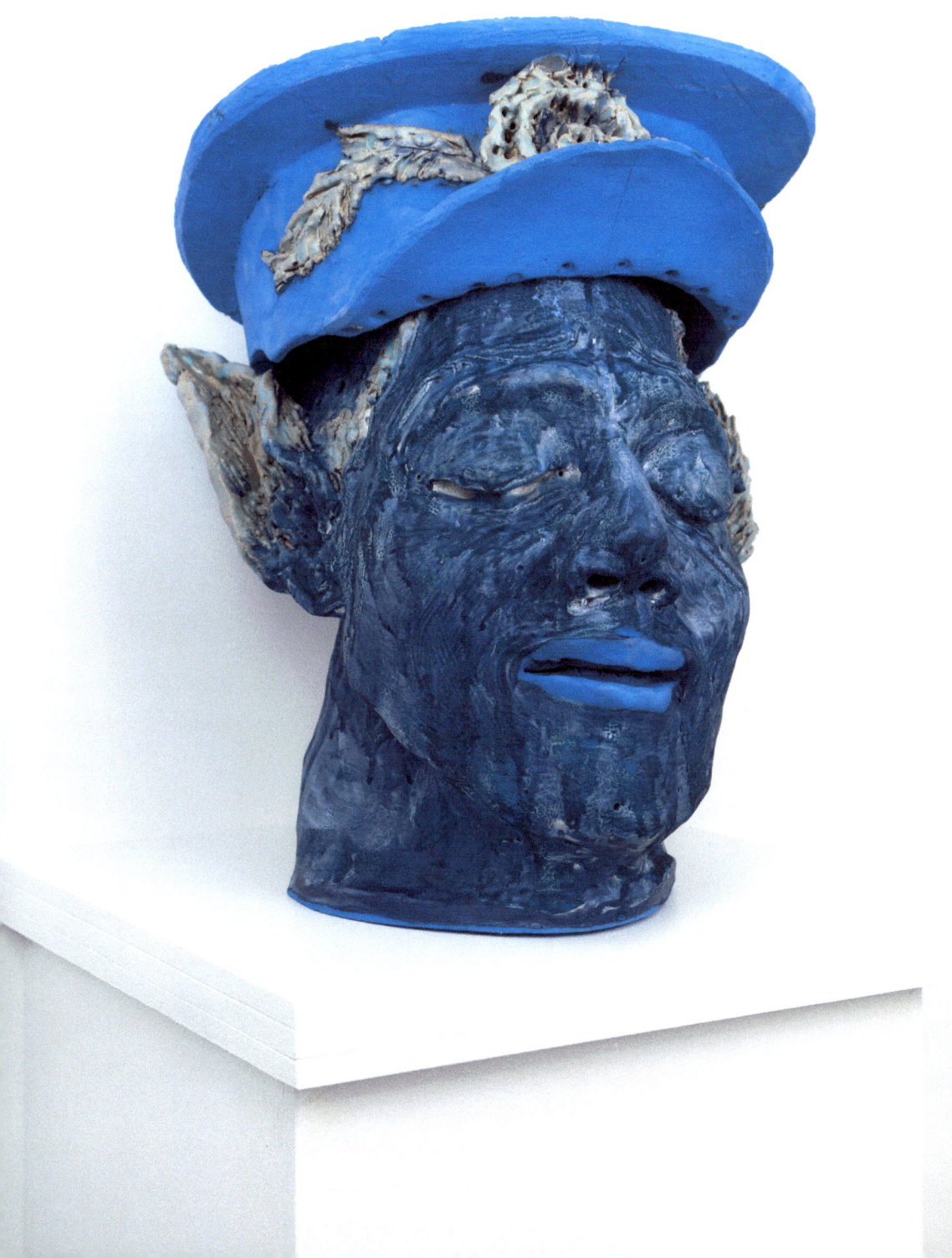

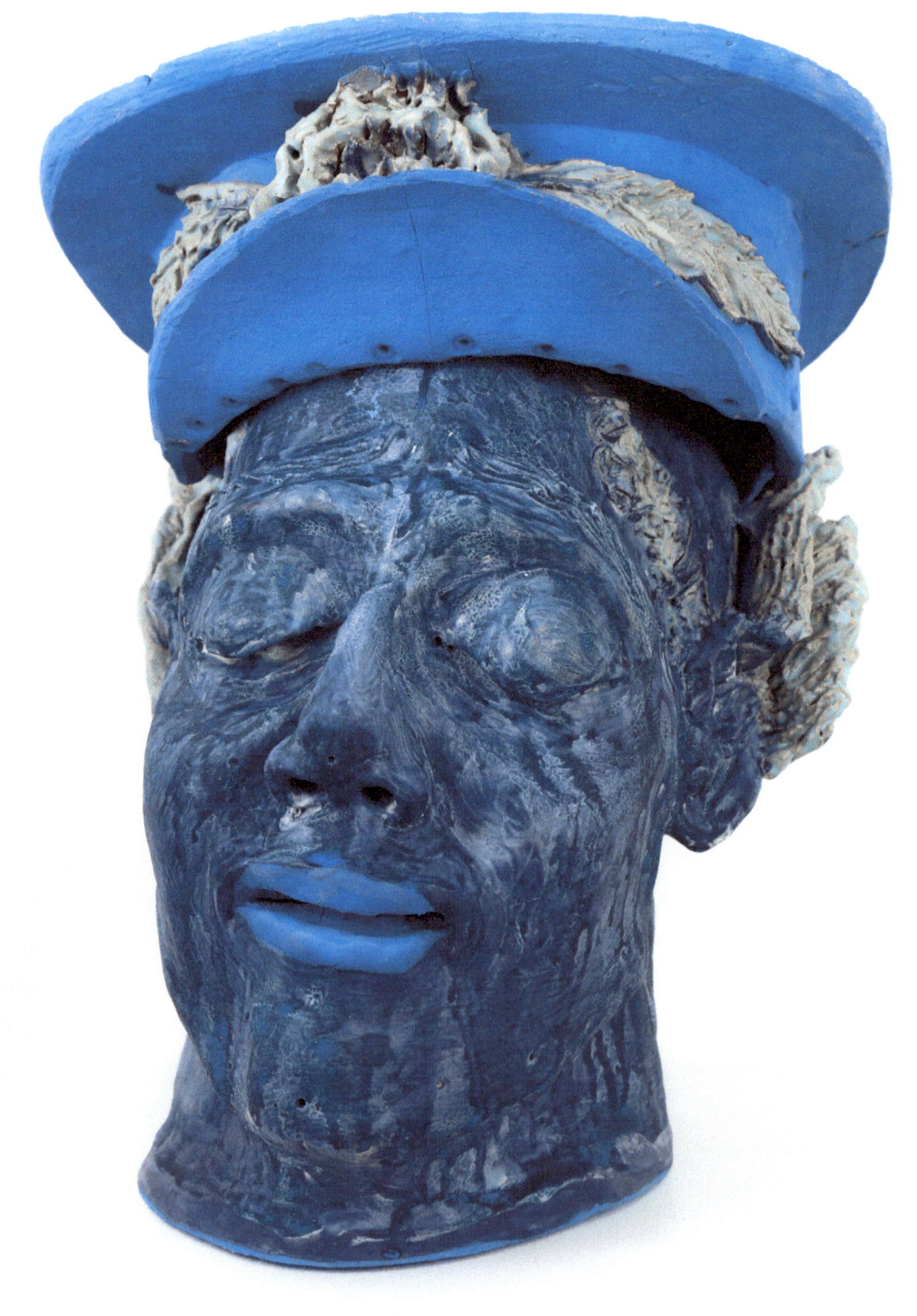

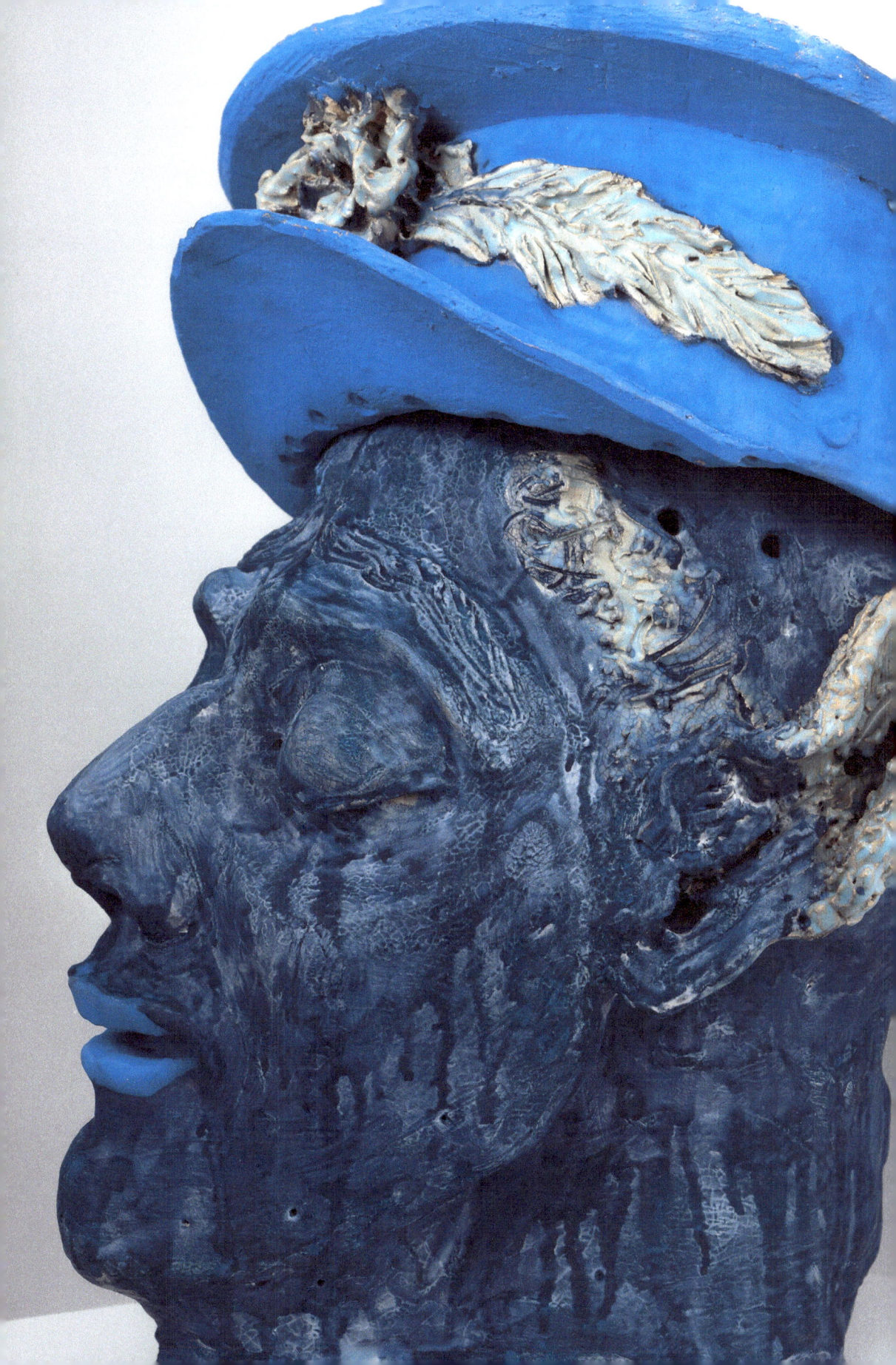

Sculptural Props from *Secret Joy*

Outside Gallery

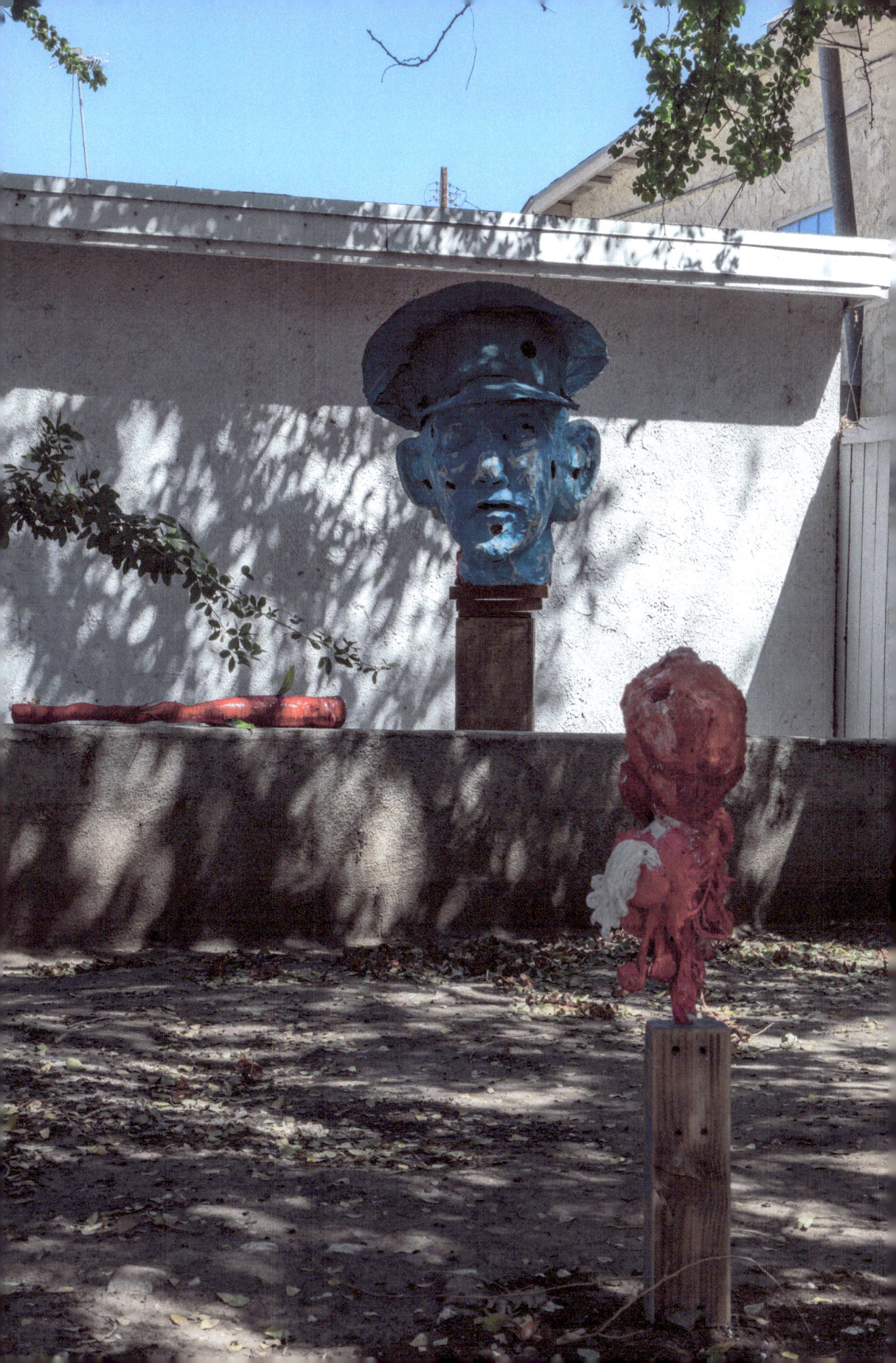

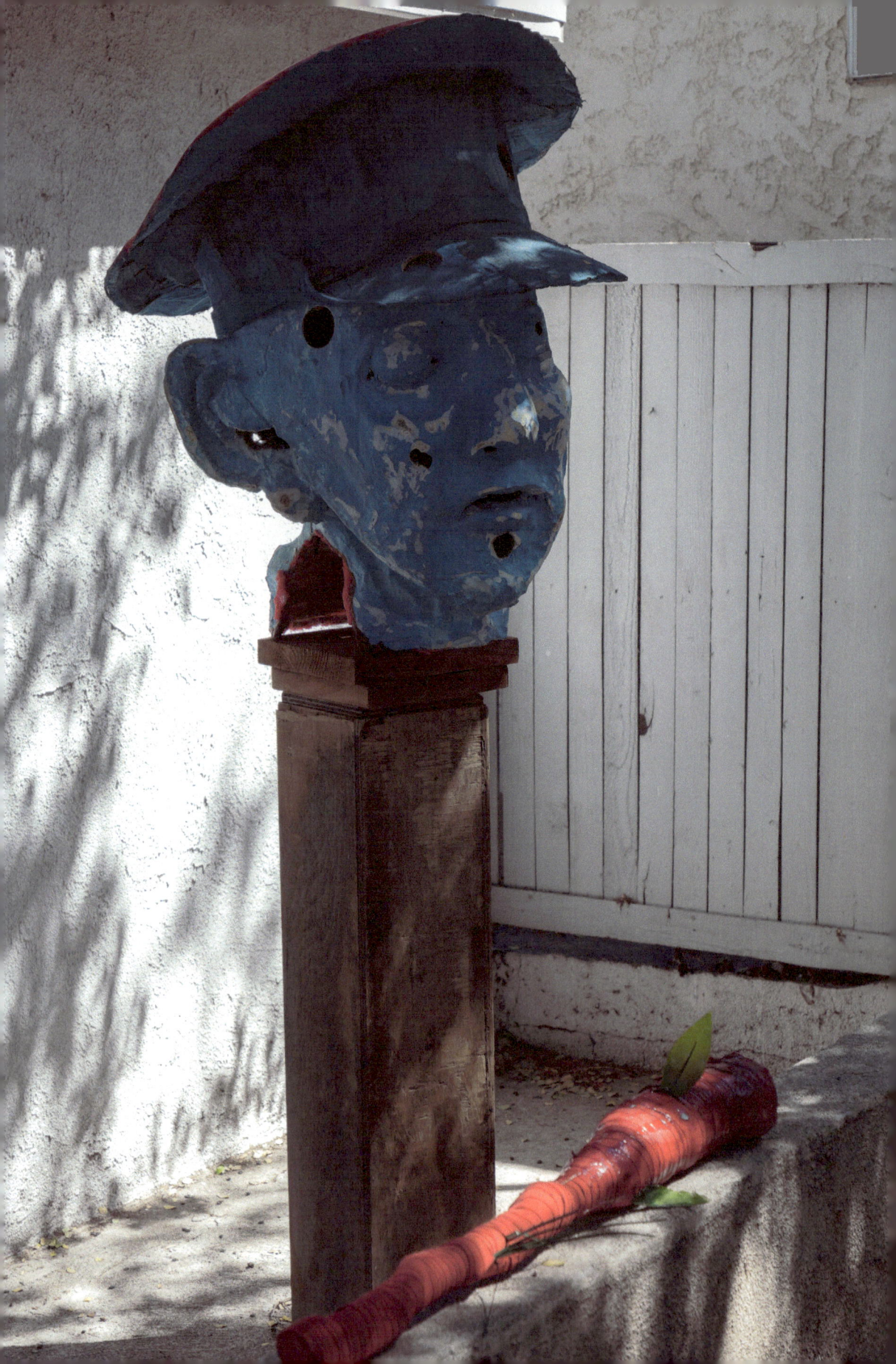

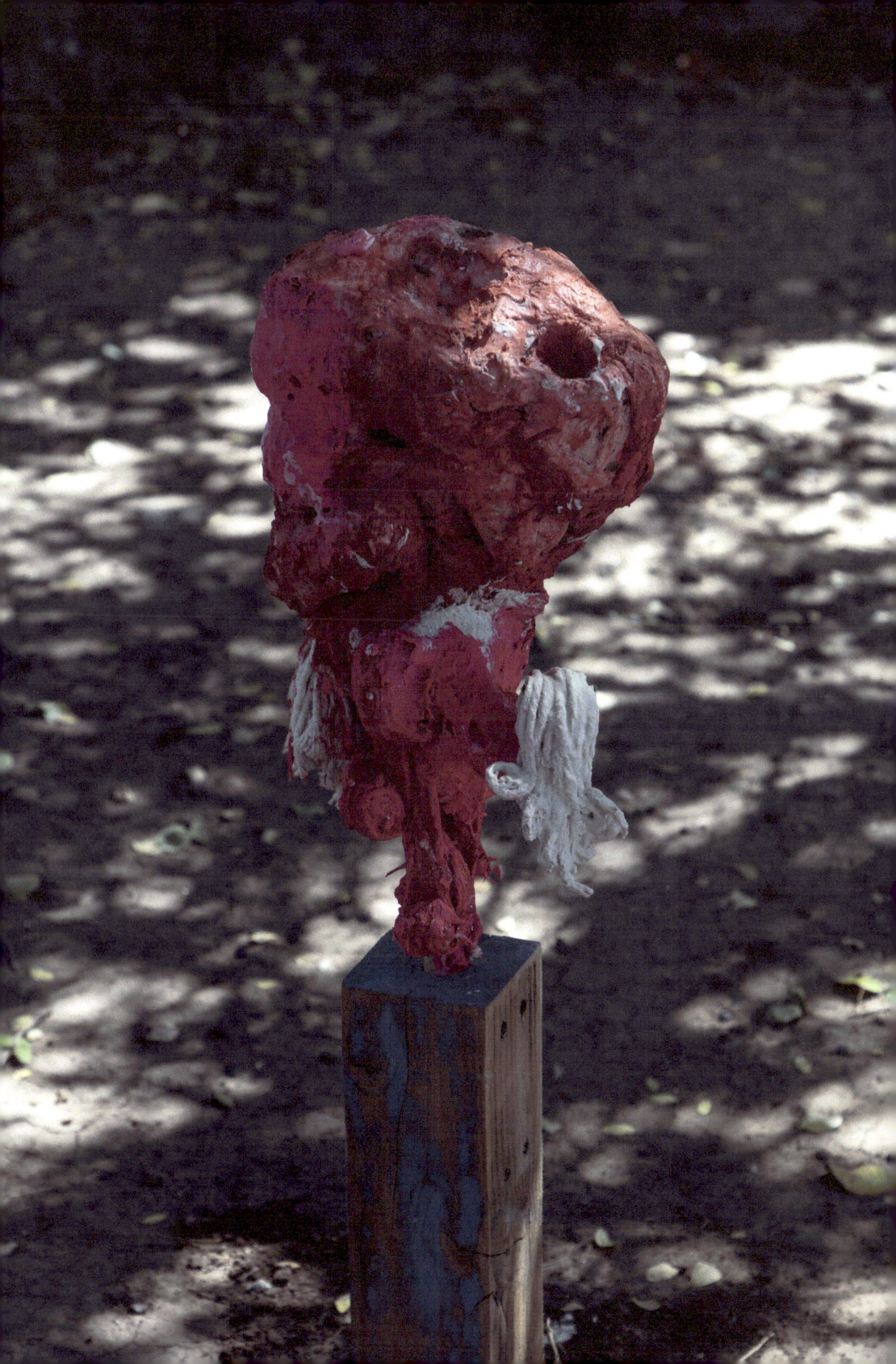

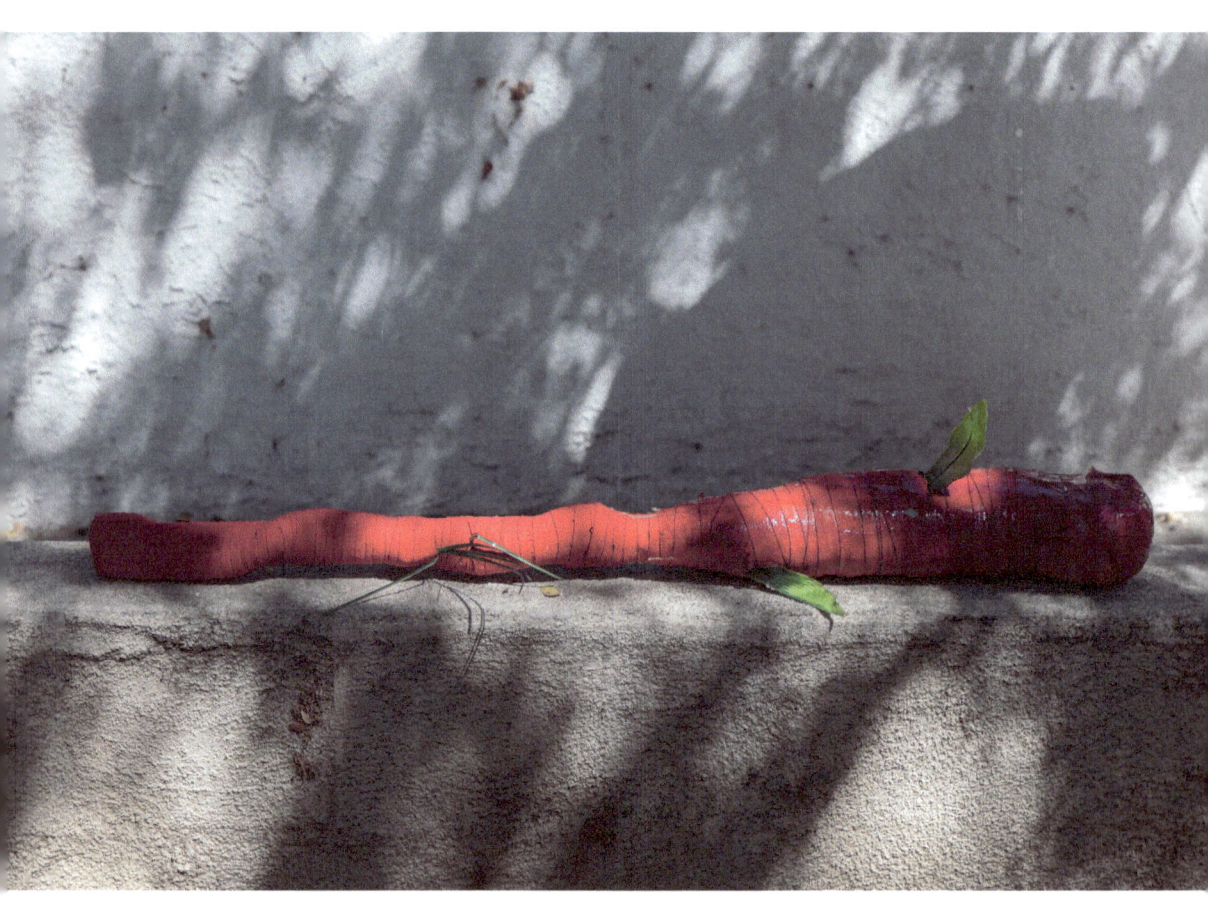

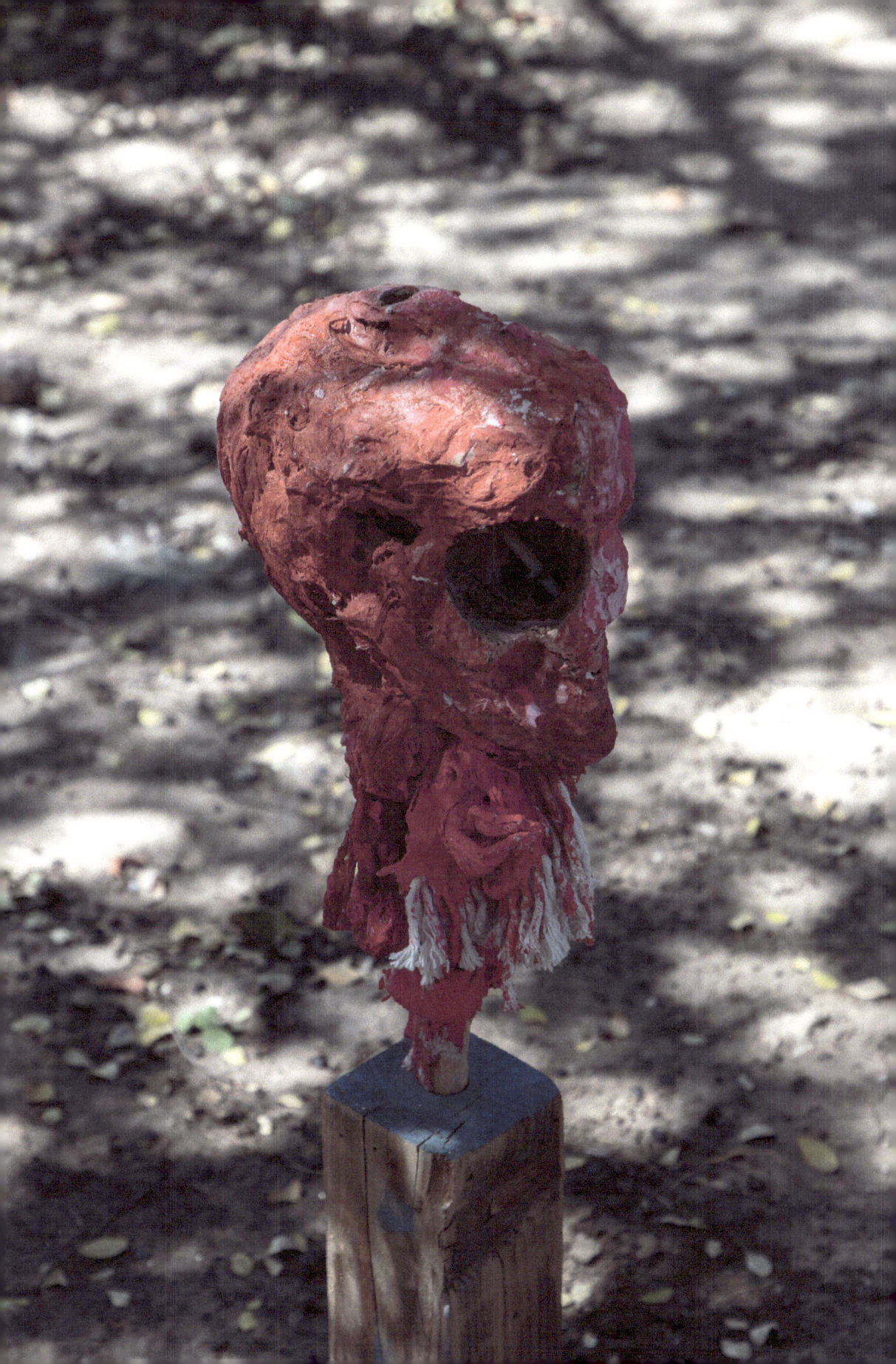

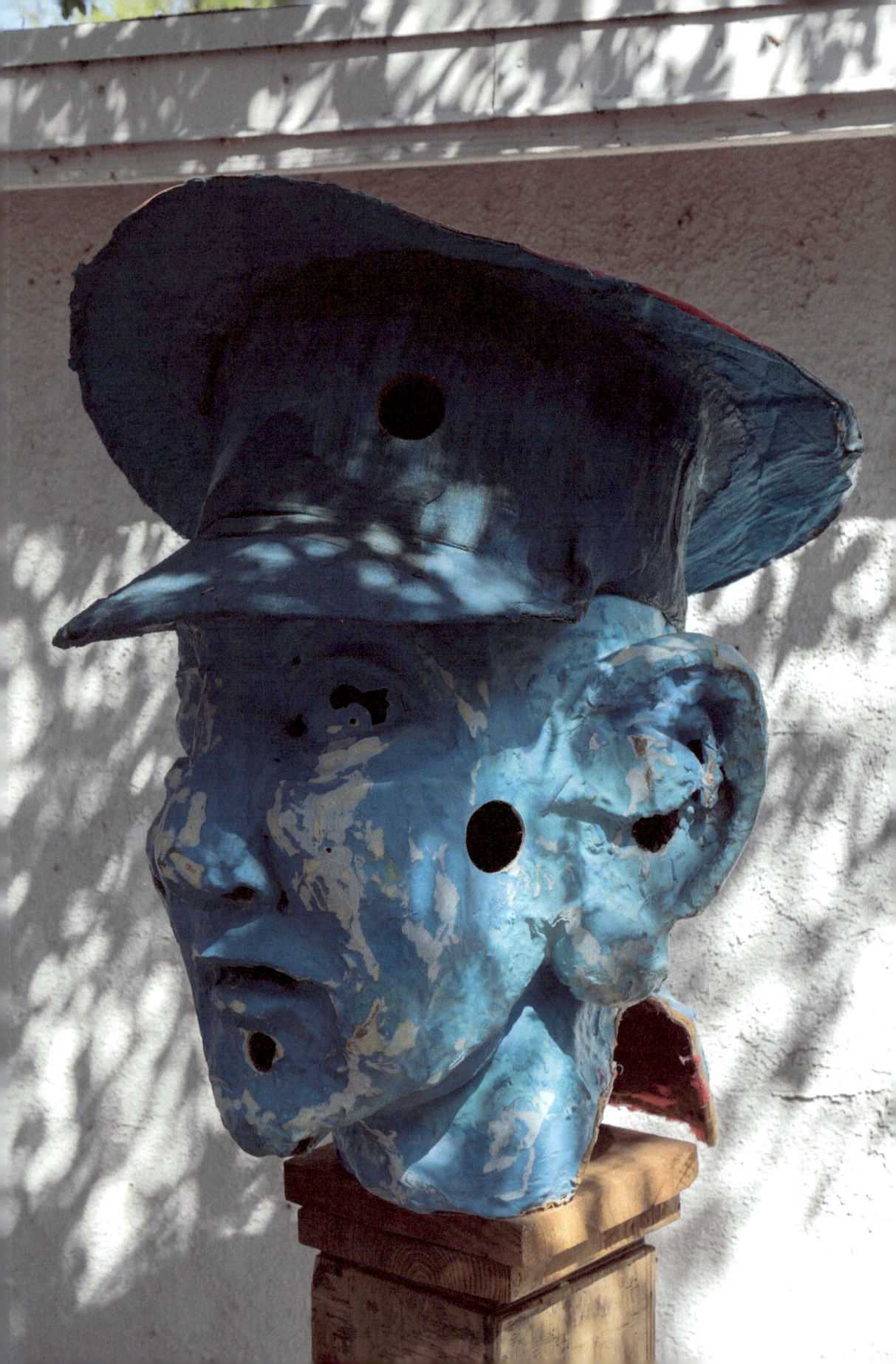

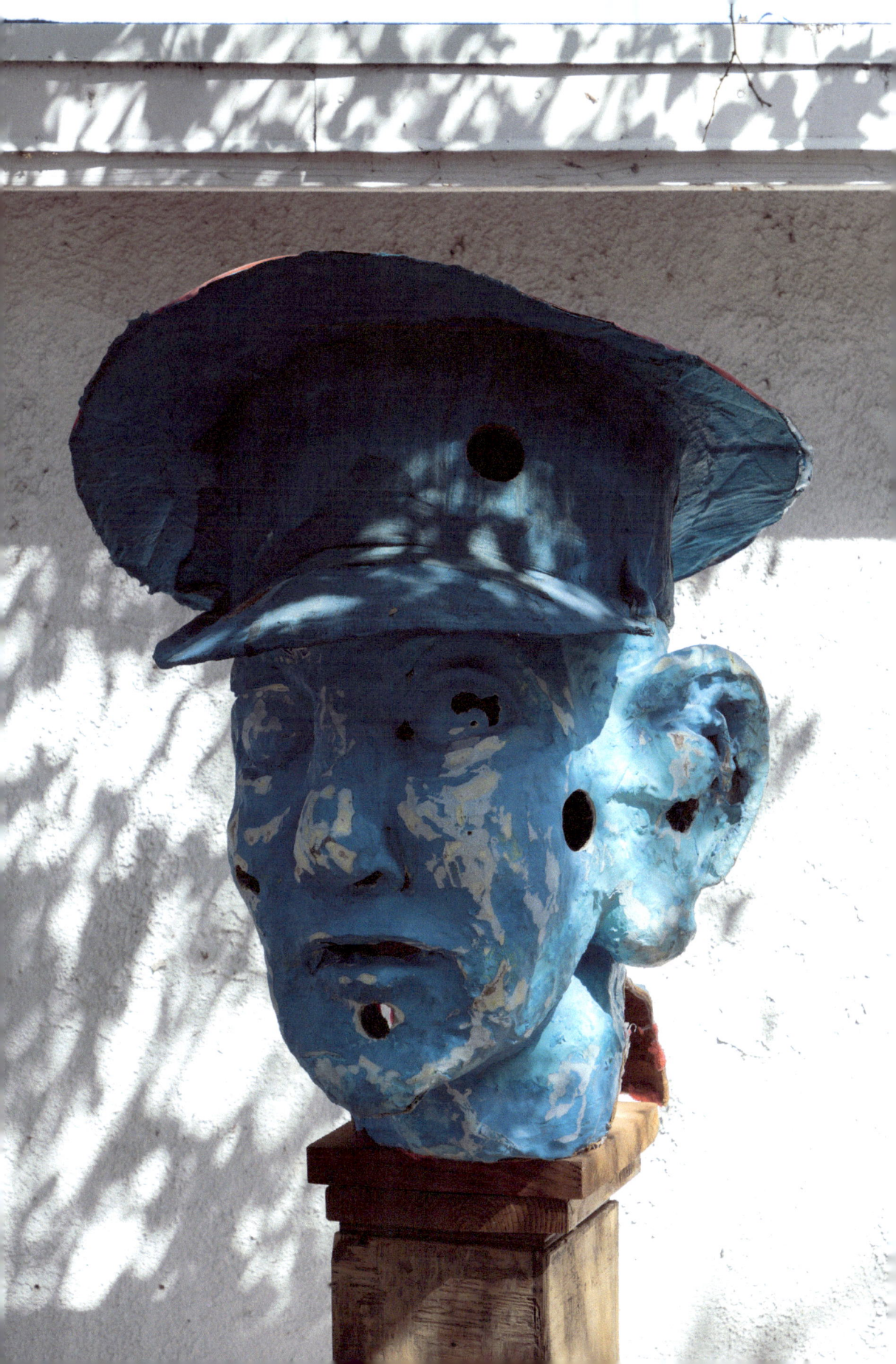

Secret Joy

performance script

Stills from the performance at
Human Resources Los Angeles 2019

Photos by Julie Weitz on pages 83, 84 and 86
and Ian Byers Gamber on pages 89, 90 and 92.

Pictured:
Dani O'Terry
Gregory Barnett

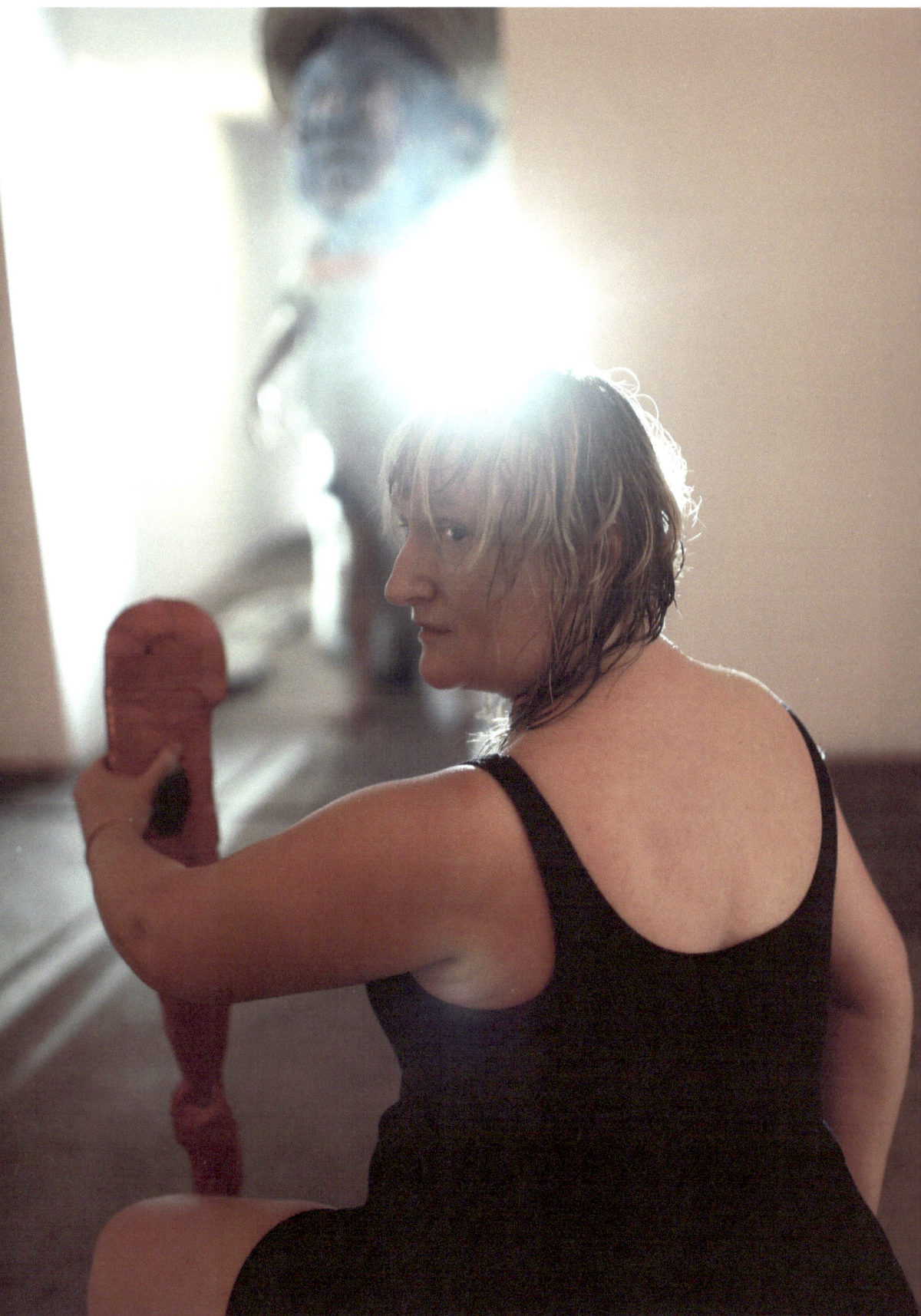

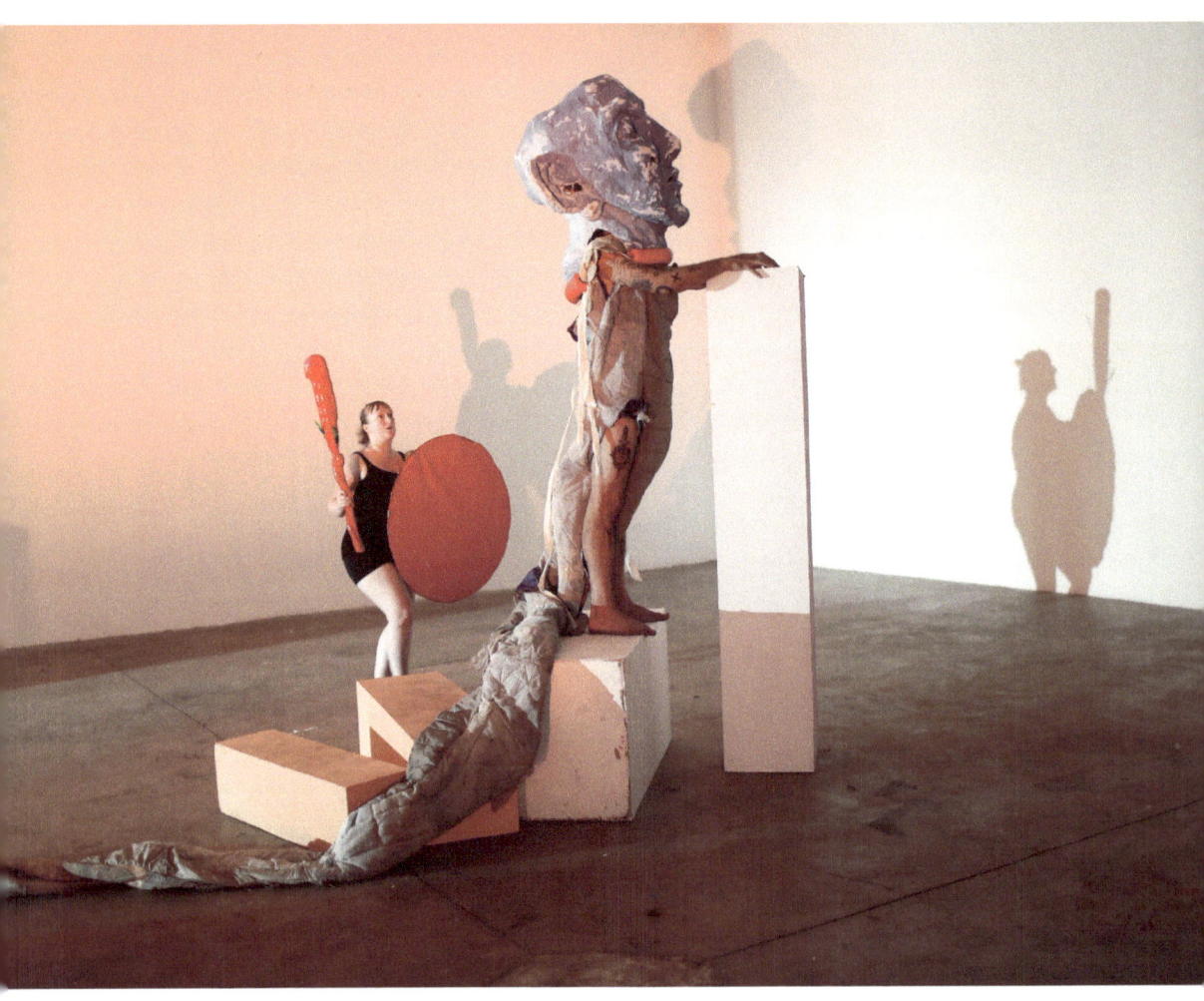

Secret Joy

excerpts from an experimental community theater production about cruelty, vacation and masks.

REY: a soldier, works with a blue monstrous soldier's head
BEA: a counter-soldier, wields a cudgel

Scene 1: Rehearse Torture, rehearse

(BEA creates a gate for REY to break, then sits on the altar)

BEA: A man came to my door
I was prepared:
Be a spider in a hole.
I was scared, I was ready to be scared
What does dread feel like?
My guts, cooking in a Pan.
I am prepared
More important
rehearse torture rehearse

(Thunderous knocking, REY wearing *the head* breaks through the gate. Chase scene, BEA hides in plain sight. REY exits. BEA resets the gate)

Repeat 4 times. BEA presents text as:
1. Memory
2. Exposition
3. Terror
4. Reversal: (Timpani. BEA finds her cudgel, beats the hat off the head, beats REY until he climbs onto the altar. REY becomes a monument. BEA becomes Perseus. Victory lap around the altar)

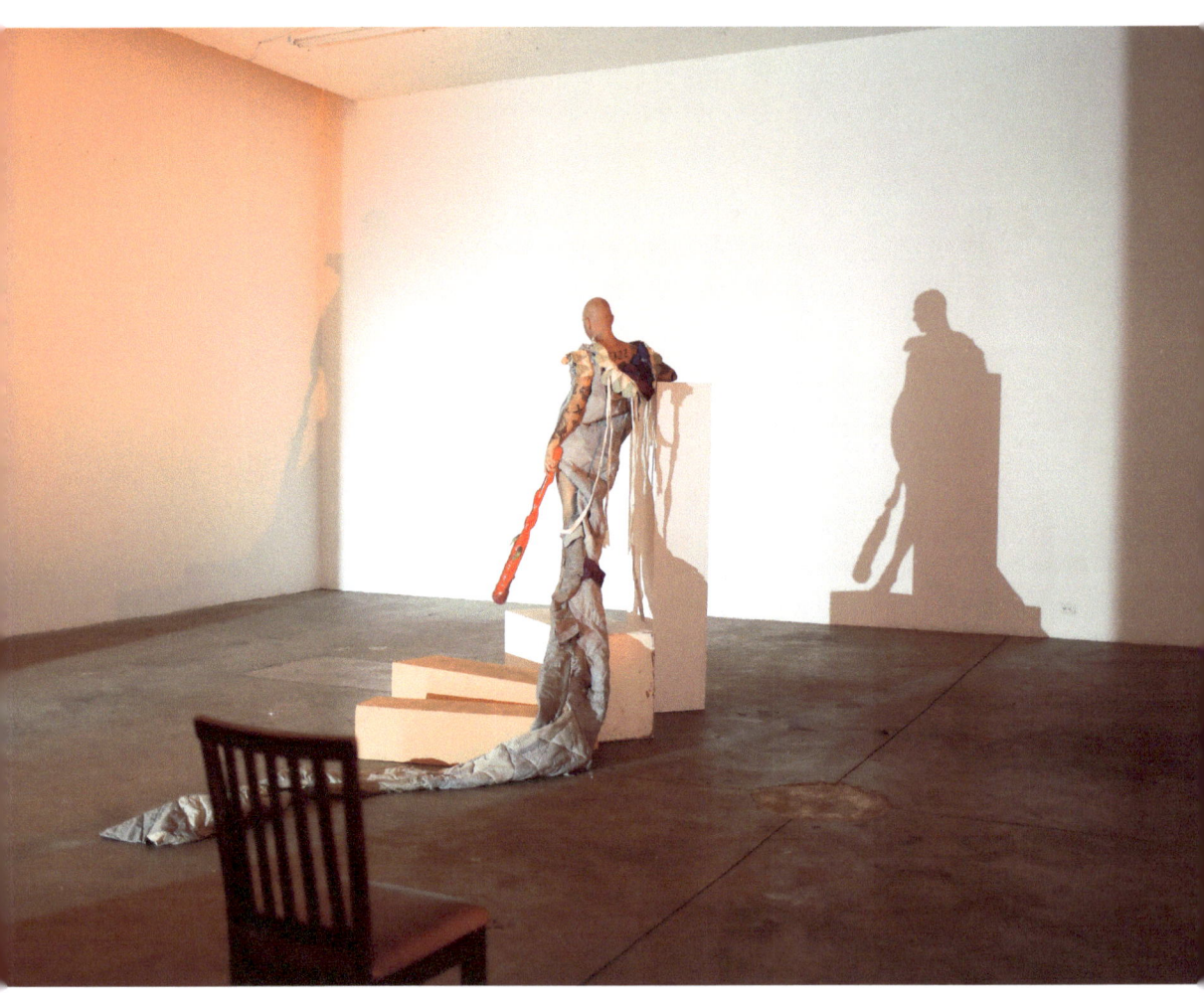

Scene 2: Vacation

(Gentle chimes. BEA and REY go to separate corners of the performance arena. Refreshments)

***

(Pachelbel's Canon in D, waves lapping. REY dones the blue head and cycles through 5 dances which BEA interprets)

BEA: I'm sorry I wasn't ready
Can you repeat that?
Repeat the sound of joy, repeat
A walk down to the peninsula intent on swimming.
Swim
Everything I need in a small bag:
snorkel and mask, a towel, sunscreen, a bottle of water.
I had a glimpse of another life:
A place to start again
The agenda so clear:
swim, drink, light candles in cold tombs.

eat drink light

Can you repeat a place?

My joy is that whole day

My whole joy day

The race to the port, foaming waves, the people moving
    across the peninsula,
I found a crevice
who would find me if a wave impaled me on the rocks
I was scared, I was really scared

satisfied and alone
having myself to myself
It was exhilarating!
I don't feel that now
So why did I return?

(BEA crowds REY's dancing)

The secret of joy
Was looking up from beneath the waves at the membrane
   between water and
Sky...breath
My secret joy was not having to choose.
Between having a body and not feeling my body at all.
The secret joy is-

(REY forces *the head* on BEA)

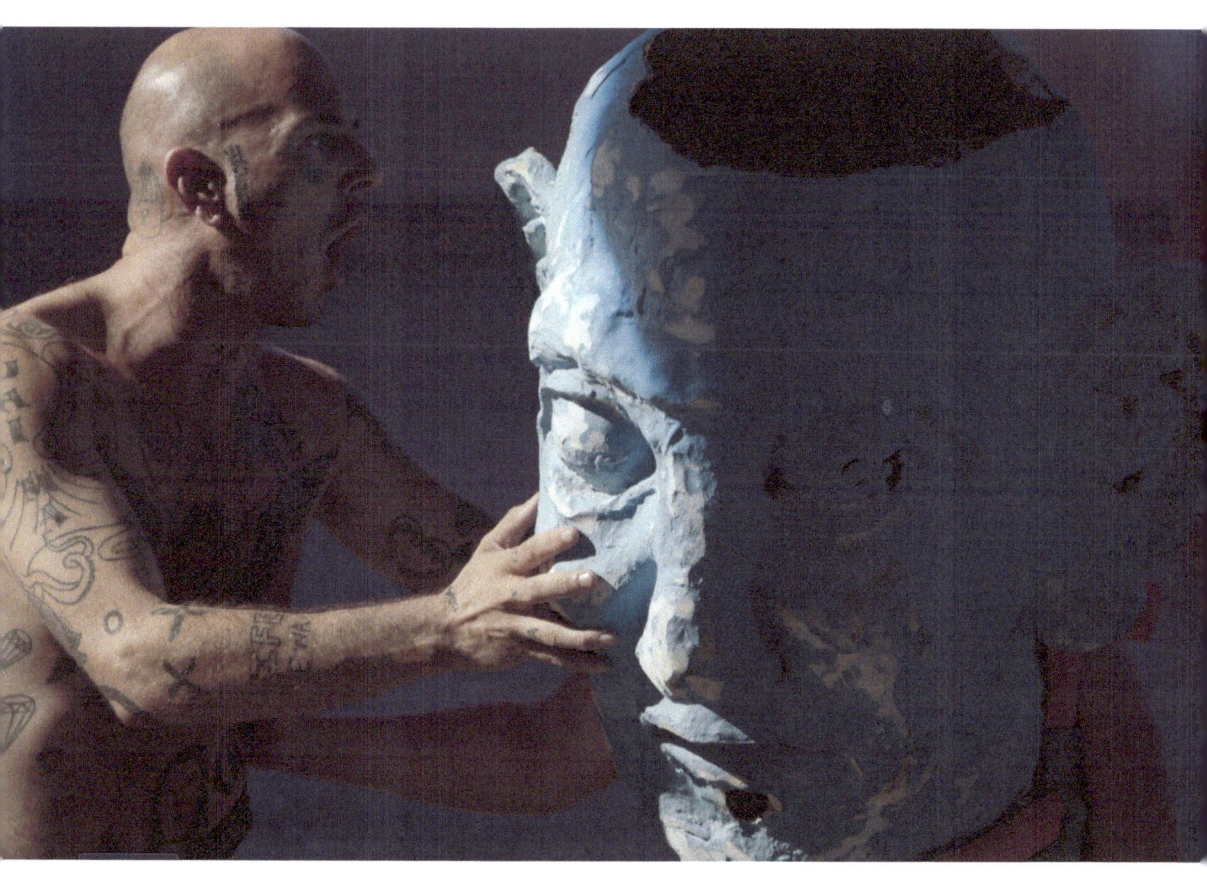

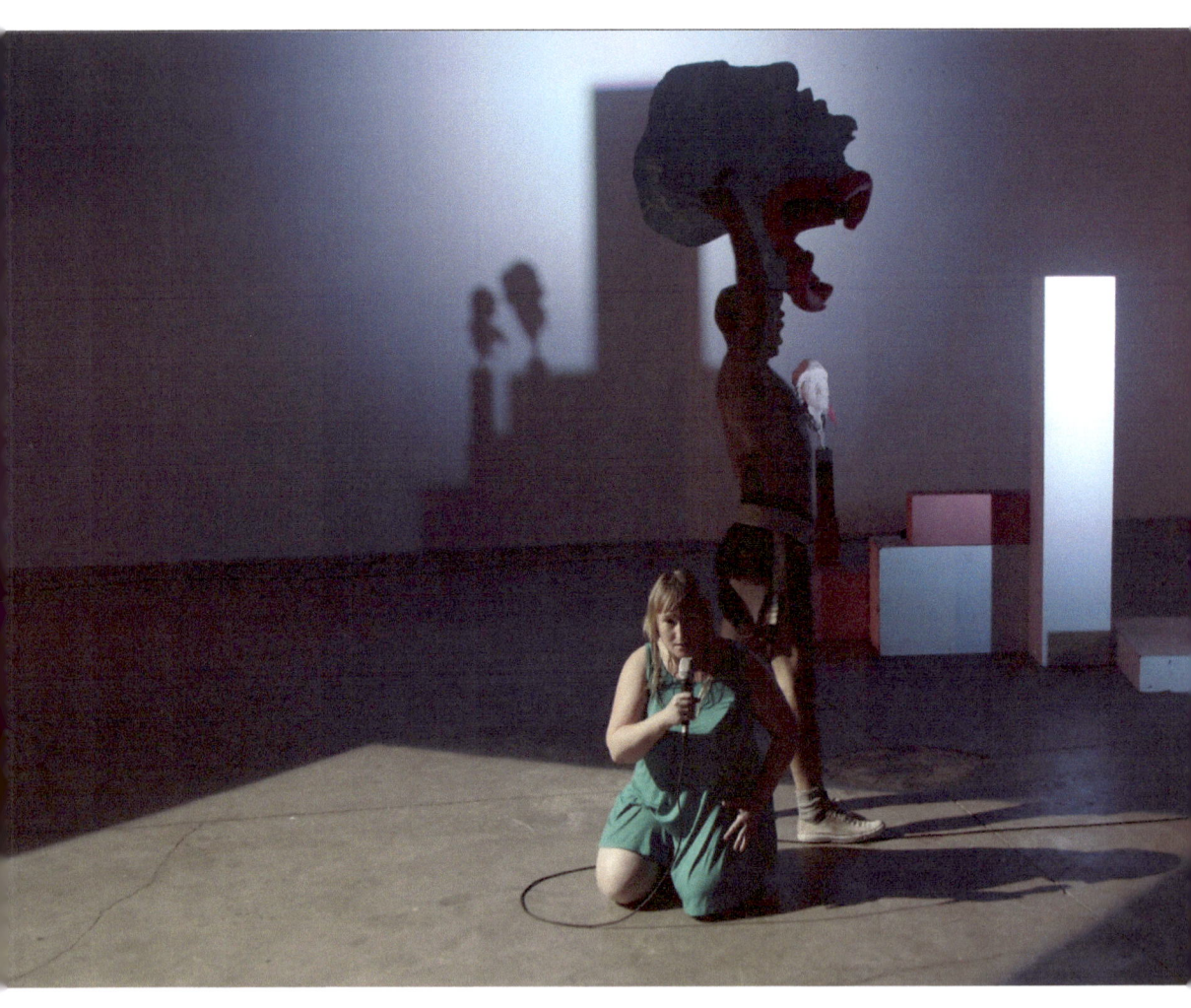

Scene 3: I make promises and break them

(Canon and waves distorted. REY 's 5 dances)

REY:
1.I don't want to lie, I don't want to lie
don't lie, don't lie

2.Dread is a finger under my rib
Pushing up with hatred
My guts in a pan.

3.Now that I'm back I'm flailing around with all
this time on my hands I'm just taking care of myself but you
      take care of everyone.
Eating low quality foods and constipated.
I tried to save my life and was punished!

4.Unbearable heart
Holding a piece of you inside, separate from your heart
hurts your body, make you sick

5(Shouted into *the head* x5) I make promises and I break them.

(BEA frees herself, REY places the head below the altar)

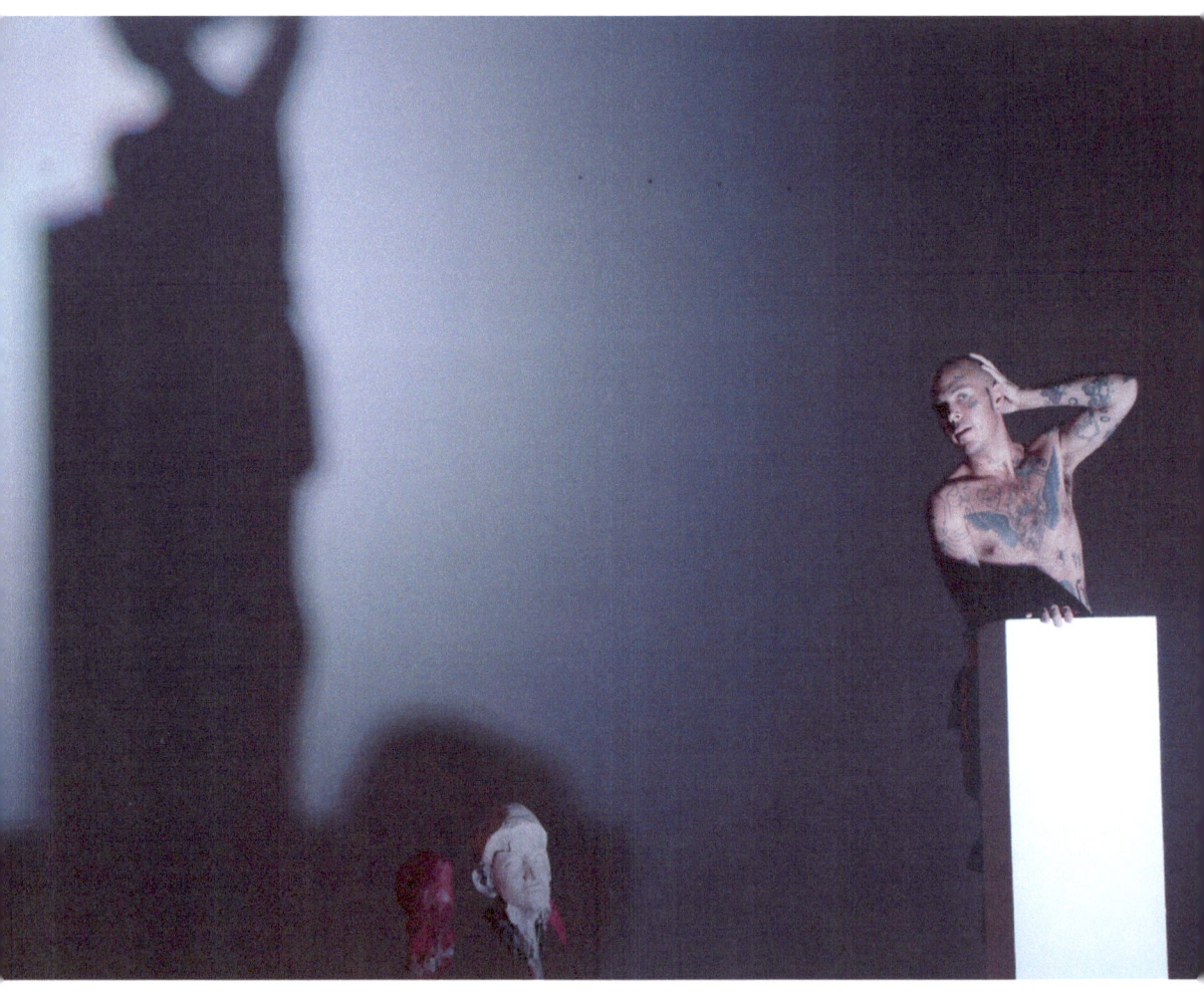

Scene 4. Kabukilini

(Hyōshigi. BEA offers up REY to the crowd. REY, on the altar, lip syncs BEA's lines like a wind up Mussolini)

BEA: A man came to my door
To beat me
To grab my hair
I got the call the day before
Someone: "you've got to leave…get your passport…go now!"

I was scared
I was really *scared*
Be a spider in a hole
I was *prepared*

I read history, it says make a trap
Keep bodies in a pit
Drag them into the street
Feed bodies to the revolution
Bodies up a line
into the sky

More important:
The rehearsals
Rehearsing their rehearsals
A creature worthy of my trap
Masks of the torturers
And if they cry…
Stay a torturer stay!

Sleep Rey,
Push your face into the ground

(Wind. REY hides his head. BEA turns *the head* on its side)

***

(Wind distorted. BEA, from behind the crowd)

Hu rah Hu rah Hu rah
Hu rah Hu rah Hu rah

(Bell, lights out, bell ringing in the dark)

***

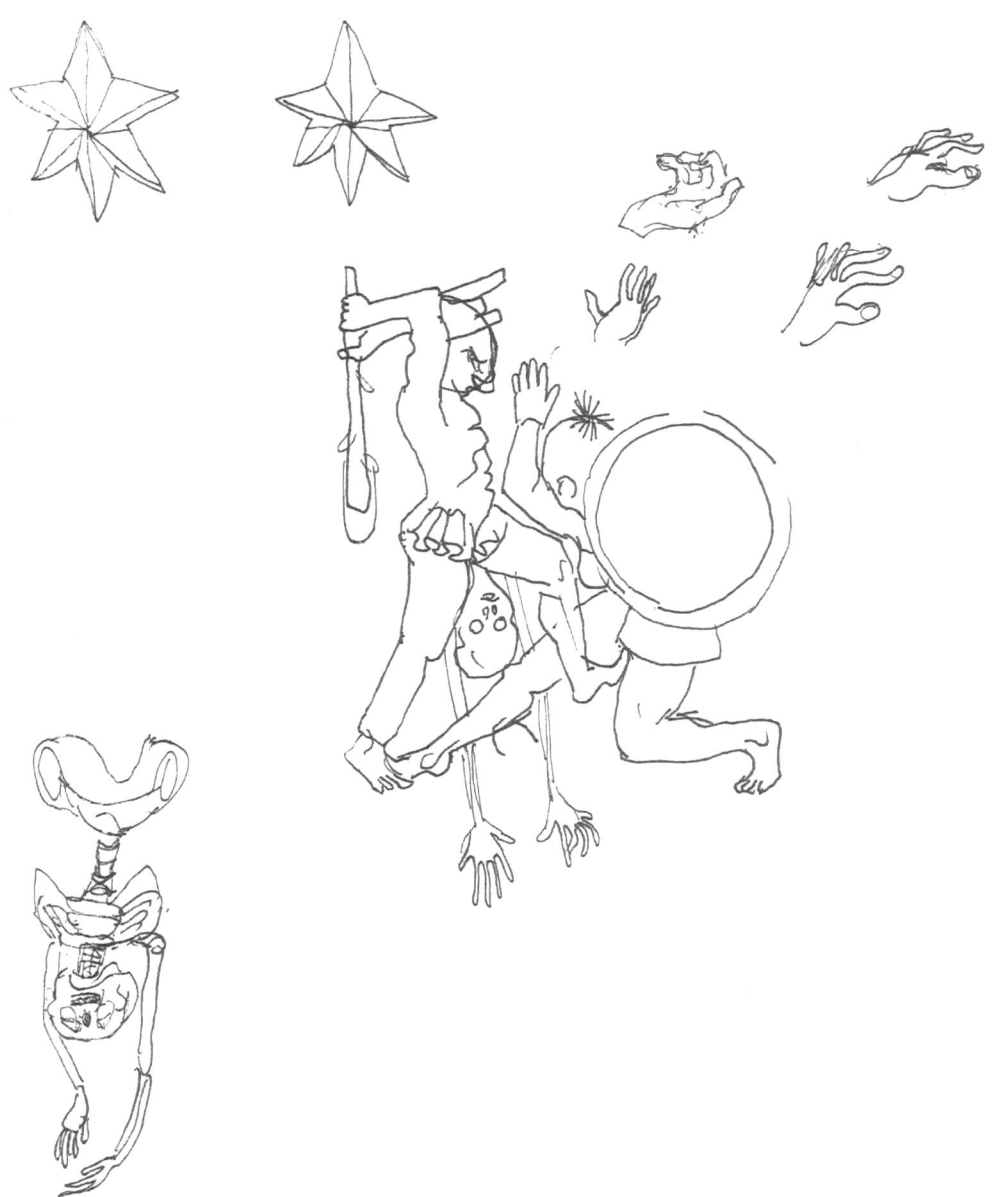

Hyper Effigy
Brian Getnick

General Projects
April 3 - May 30, 2021

Press Release
and
Index of Works

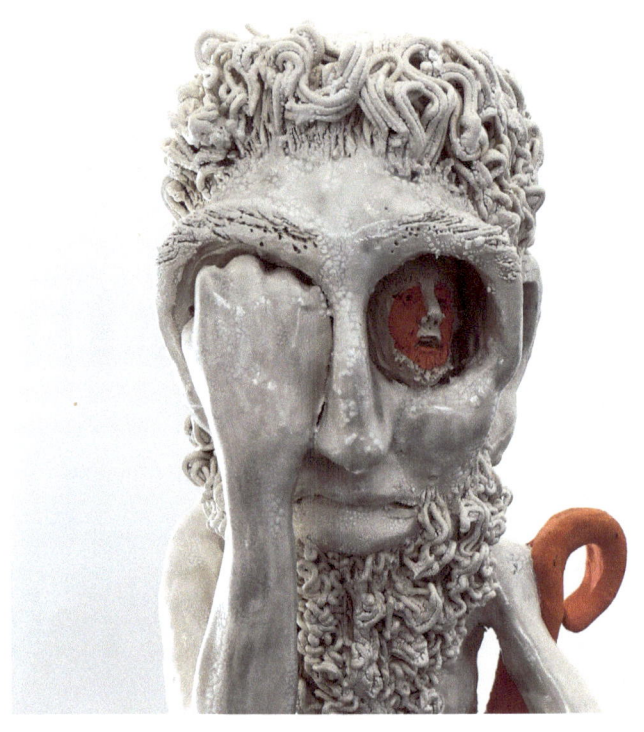

GENERAL PROJECTS

A division of Insert Blanc Press   insertblancpress.net

Brian Getnick
Hyper Effigy

General Projects
3611 Pomona St.
Los Angeles, CA 90031

April 3, 2021 - May 30, 2021

Opening by appointment April 3 form 4-9pm

Open Hours by appointment Thursdays 7-9pm

Insert Blanc Press is pleased to present **Hyper Effigy**, a new exhibition by Brian Getnick at General Projects & Outside Gallery.

In Brian Getnick's new body of work, he offers two sculptural investigations of icons associated with fascism, terrorism, and the pre-modern past. "Ersatz Fighting Unit" draws inspiration from the 20th century interwar period and features a blue officer (sprouting donkey ears) facing off against a red balaclava wearing revolutionary. In "Abyss Standard" ancestral faces and dream entities merge in statuettes radially arranged to mark a weekly cycle of Trumpian era crisis. In Hyper Effigy, Getnick forwards caricature as a magical language; a grammar of soldiers, trolls, terrorists and skeletons, equipped to dislodge propagandistic representations of the *other* from their historical ideological functions.

On display in Outside Gallery are a monumental soldier's head, a cudgel and a red medusa; sculptural props from "Secret Joy", a performance Getnick directed in 2019 after a journey to Eastern Europe*.

Time slots are limited to four people max every 30 minutes. Please wear masks and maintain spatial distance of 6 feet or more. Please honor the time slot you have signed up for as RSVPs are limited. General Projects is located in a converted garage accessible via a small ramp and one step thru a 35 inch wide doorway.

* travel and research in Eastern Europe for "Secret Joy" and "Ersatz Fighting Unit" was facilitated by the Yiddishkayt Helix Fellowship.

Thursday, Abyss Standard
2021, 18" x 8" x 8"
Glazed Ceramic

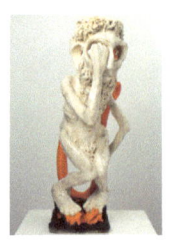

Friday, Abyss Standard
2021, 17" x 6" x 6"
Glazed Ceramic

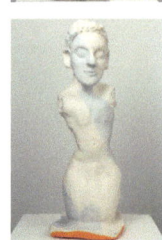

Saturday, Abyss Standard
2021, 18" x 10" x 7"
Glazed Ceramic

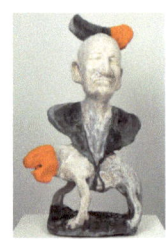

Sunday, Abyss Standard
2021, 18" x 9" x 6"
Glazed Ceramic

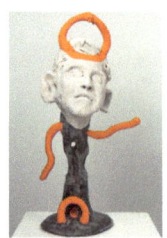

Monday, Abyss Standard
2021, 18" x 8" x 6"
Glazed Ceramic

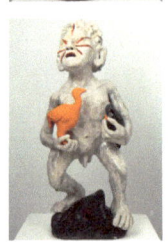

Tuesday, Abyss Standard
2021, 19" x 11" x 7"
Glazed Ceramic

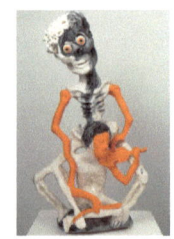

Wednesday, Abyss Standard
2021, 15" x 10" x 7"
Glazed Ceramic

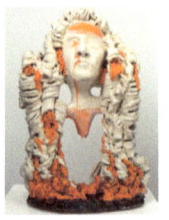

Coin
2021, 26" x 26"
mixed media on paper

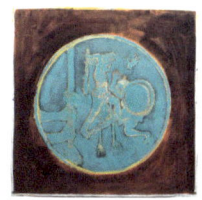

Blue Way
2021, 39" x 36"
mixed media on paper

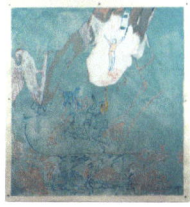

Red Way
2021, 36" x 39"
mixed media on paper

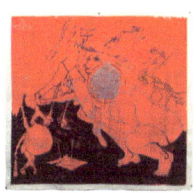

**Soldier,
Ersatz Fighting Unit**
2021, 17" x 14" x 16"
Glazed Ceramic

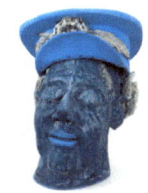

**Counter Soldier,
Ersatz Fighting Unit**
2021, 15" x 8" x 10"
Glazed Ceramic

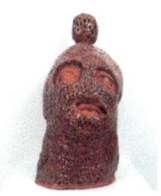

**Soldier / Counter Soldier,
Ersatz Fighting Unit**
2021, 21" x 8" x 8"
Glazed Cermic

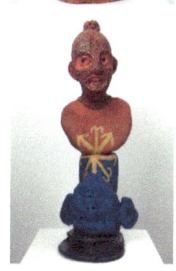

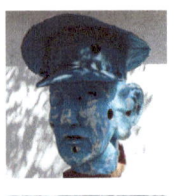
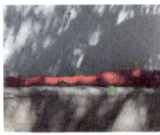
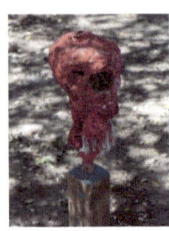

Outside Gallery

sculptural props from
Secret Joy

*Drawings from
Brian Getnick's sketchbook
pages: 10, 13-19, 22, 49, 96, 103.*

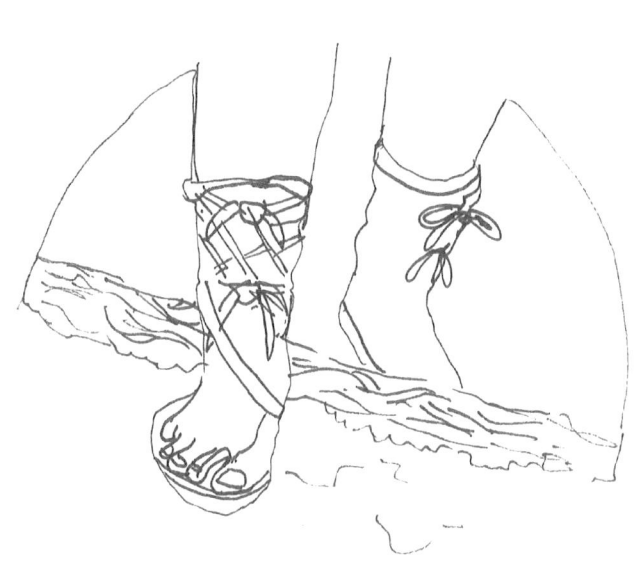

www.ingramcontent.com/pod-product-compliance
Lightning Source LLC
Chambersburg PA
CBHW040058250526
45473CB00044B/2398